T0208133

Practical Taoism

Practical Taoism

Translated by THOMAS CLEARY

SHAMBHALA
Boulder
1996

SHAMBHALA PUBLICATIONS, INC.
2129 13th Street
Boulder, Colorado 80302
www.shambhala.com

Printed in the United States of America

Shambhala Publications makes every effort to print on acid-
free, recycled paper.

Shambhala Publications is distributed worldwide by Penguin
Random House, Inc., and its subsidiaries.

LIBRARY OF CONGRESS CATALOGING-IN-PUBLICATION DATA

Practical Taoism/translated by Thomas Cleary.
    p. cm.
    A translation of traditional writings and classical
commentary on Taoist meditation practices.
    ISBN 978-1-57062-200-7 (alk. paper)
    1. Hygiene, Taoist. 2. Taoism. I. Cleary, Thomas.
RA781.P667 1996   95-23894
613—dc20   CIP

BVG 01

Contents

Contents

Translator's Preface

Taoism, the original wisdom tradition of ancient China, may be rendered in English as "Wayfaring." In this manner of usage, the Way is classically defined in these terms: "Humanity follows earth, earth follows heaven, heaven follows the Way, the Way follows Nature." In the final sense, therefore, Taoism, or Wayfaring, refers to the pursuit of natural laws.

These natural laws are reflected in the body (earth), the mind (heaven), and in the order of the universe (the Way of Nature). The practice of Taoism, therefore, takes place in the cultivation and refinement of the natural capacities of the human body-mind continuum and its relationship with the social milieu and the natural world.

Taoist pursuit of natural laws extends beyond those recognized within a limited cultural context, seeking to uncover and activate latent sensitivities that enable the individual to enter into an increasingly intimate, vitalizing, inspiring relationship with Life in all of its manifestations.

According to classical tradition, Taoism cannot be encompassed within just one framework of expression. As a result of this particular quality, many diverse modes of Taoist activity emerged over the centuries. One of the most popular of these is the science of inner alchemy, which energizes the body and purifies the mind, thus producing a transmutation in consciousness enhancing the individual experience of life.

There are two main sourcebooks of internal alchemy, known as the Ancestors of Alchemical Treatises: *Triplex Unity,* by the second century CE adept Wei Boyang, and *Understanding Reality,* by the eleventh century CE adept Zhang Ziyang. Couched in cryptic symbolic language, these two texts spawned a great deal of commentary and not a little controversy. Eventually the opacity of alchemical terminology led some Taoist writers to adopt more explicit manners of expression in order to enable seekers to put the teachings into practice.

The present text is one such work, a collection of quotations from alchemical classics along with practical explanations by expert Taoists. It is attributed to a seventh generation master of the Northern Branch of the Complete Reality School of Taoism, known as the Preserver of Truth. It contains sayings of many famous adepts, devoted specifically to elucidating the modes and manners of practical Wayfaring represented by the mysteries of spiritual alchemy.

Practical Taoism

Introduction

There are two ways of cultivating refinement. The *Classic of Wenshi* says, "If you can see the vital spirit, you gain lasting life; if you can forget the vital spirit, you gain transcendent life."

Forgetting the vital spirit means emptiness climaxes, quietude is attained, and vitality naturally transmutes into energy, energy naturally transmutes into spirit, and spirit naturally returns to emptiness. This is the study of the Great Way of absolute nonresistance.

Seeing the vital spirit means taking emptiness and quietude for substance, the firing process for function, refining vitality into energy, refining energy into spirit, and refining spirit back into emptiness. This is the study of driving energy by spirit.

Although the study of the Great Way of absolute nonresistance does not touch on vitality and energy, still one merges in reality with the Way, physically and mentally sublimated, appearing and disappearing in being and nonbeing, changing unfathomably, with a life span that is measureless. This is comprehending essence and then spontaneously comprehending life. This is including the lower in the higher.

Using spirit to drive energy involves vitality and energy, but one preserves their original harmony, working unceasingly. The ultimate harmony permeates and sublimates, producing liquid fluidity that can also make the physical unite with the spiritual to live without dying. This is comprehending life, with essence thereby abiding. This is progressing to the higher from the lower.

The Great Way of absolute nonresistance applies to the metaphysical body; driving energy by means of spirit applies to the physical body. Although these two are different in magnitude, nevertheless they are the realities of spiritual alchemy, the true source of the Great Way; there is benefit in realizing them, and they can be accomplished by practice. They are not like the minor arts of auxiliary methods, at which one may labor without accomplishing anything.

When I first met my teacher long ago, I asked for instruction on learning immortality. My teacher said that learning immortality may be artificial or real: the artificial is the way of the methodologists, while the real is the way of the wayfarers. Subsequently receiving instruction, fortunately I was able to transcend the ordinary. Now then, the arts of methodologists are such as consumption of the seeds of plants and trees and the essences of metals and minerals, and methods of culling yin to augment yang. The way of wayfarers consists of two points: forgetting the vital spirit and seeing the vital spirit.

Those who seek eternal life by techniques will inevitably ruin their own lives. Going by the Way, however, one will not only live long but also directly experience birthlessness. There is a great difference between the real and the artificial, the Way and techniques; those with perception will be able to distinguish them on their own.

Since olden times, however, there have been many Taoist books in which ancient teachers set up all sorts of similes, using objects to stand for terms, using terms to lodge meanings. This is because the true Way is hard to express, so they wanted to present clues without speaking clearly. That is all there is to it, but later students nevertheless got mired in words and clung to abstract metaphors.

If you let go of things, your body is not stressed; if you contrive no artificiality, your mind is naturally at peace. Serenity and lightness develop day by day, while involvement in objects grows thinner day by day. Your actions become further and further from mundanity, while your mind becomes closer and closer to the Way.

Some people display virtue and show ability in order to get others to support them. Some call on people for celebrations and funerals, in effect making business trips. Some affect seclusion as hermits but are actually seeking social advancement. Some offer people food and drink in hopes of later favors. All of these are clever operations of the crafty mind for gaining temporal profit. These prevent right action and so should all be abandoned.

As long as you do not start anything, others will not join in; even if others do start something, you do not join in. Gradually cutting off old entanglements, do not form new entanglements.

Foods include wine and meat; clothing includes fine silks; social status includes reputation and position; material wealth includes gold and jade; but these luxuries are all excesses of emotional desires, not good medicines that enhance life. People who pursue them bring about their own destruction. How confused can you get!

The second thing is to govern the mind. The mind is the ruler of the whole body, the commander of all the mental powers. When it is quiet, it produces insight; when agitated, it becomes unclear. Therefore, in the beginning of study of the Way, it is necessary to sit calmly, collect the mind, and detach from objects, so the mind does not possess anything. By dwelling in nonpossession, one does not cling to anything, spontaneously entering into absolute nonresistance. The mind then merges with the Way.

As for the source of the substance of mind, its root is the Way; but because the mind gets stained and obscured, it gradually becomes vagrant, eventually becoming estranged from the Way. If you clean the pollution from the mind and open up consciousness of the root of the spirit, that is called practicing the Way.

When the mind no longer wanders vagrant but merges with the Way and rests calmly in the Way, that is called return to the root. Keeping to the root without straying is called serene stabilization. Over a long time at this, diseases vanish, life returns, returns and continues, so you naturally come to know the eternal. Knowing means nothing is obscure; eternal means there is no change. Emancipation from birth and death really comes from here.

If you want to cultivate reality, first get rid of warped behaviors. With external affairs cut off, there is nothing to concern the mind; after that, you gaze inwardly with precise awareness. When you notice a thought arising, eliminate it. Eliminate thoughts as they arise, in order to bring about peaceful calmness.

Next, even if you don't actually have any obsessive fixations, floating random thoughts should also be eliminated. Practicing diligently day and night, not deviating for a moment, just extinguish the stirring mind, do not extinguish the shining mind; just accord with the open mind, not with the possessive mind. Then the mind does not depend on anything but always abides in truth.

To pacify and stabilize the mind, it is important to have no obsessions. If you dwell on openness, emptiness, or nonresistance with a clinging mind, this is still possessiveness, not nonpossessiveness. To abide in possessiveness causes the mind to toil; it is out of harmony with truth, and also produces sickness. As long as the mind does not dwell on anything and is imperturbable, this is authentic stability and accurate awareness. Use this for stabilization, and mind and mood will be in tune, becoming lighter and airier as time goes on. When you use this as a test, right and wrong become obvious.

Above the stabilized mind is vast openness, with no covering; beneath the stabilized mind is open vastness, with no dependency.

Eliminate confusion without extinguishing perception; maintain calmness without sticking to emptiness. Practice this consistently, and you will naturally attain true vision.

Whether the mind is ordinarily hyperactive or calm is a matter of long-term habit; it is very hard to have the discipline to stop the mind. One may try to stop it and yet be unable, or one may manage to do so temporarily and then lose it. The whole body flows with sweat under the duress of the struggle between losing and keeping; only after a long, long process of softening does one finally attain mature attunement. Do not give up your regular practice because of temporary failure to collect the mind.

Once you have attained some calmness, then you should consciously stabilize it at all times, whether working or still, sitting or reclining—even when dealing with things in the midst of clamor. Whether there is something to attend to or nothing to attend to, always be as if unminding; whether in quietude or in clamor, let your will remain unified.

The mind has been resting on objects all along, and so it is not used to independence; suddenly without resort, it is hard for it to remain at rest spontaneously. Even if you can pacify it for a while, it scatters in confusion again. Govern it as it arises, so that it does not become agitated. Eventually, after a long time, it will become tuned and tamed, able to be at peace naturally and spontaneously. Day or night, whatever you may be doing, always consciously stabilize it; if your mind attains stability, then you must nurture it calmly not allowing any annoyance. When you have attained some peace, then you can enjoy yourself, gradually becoming accustomed to it, becoming increasingly pure and aloof.

If things sometimes give rise to doubts, then for the time being do all the thinking you need to solve the matter, and you will also come to understand what you have wondered about. This is also an authentic root of wisdom. Once you have understood, stop and don't think anymore; if you keep on thinking, your intellect will damage your essence, ruining the principal for the sake of the interest. Even if you develop outstanding cleverness for a time, ultimately that will compromise long-term work.

If you are afflicted by false and random thoughts, abandon them as you become aware of them; if you hear criticism or praise, good or bad, ignore it all and don't take it into your mind. If you take it in, your mind will be filled; if your mind is filled, there's no room for the Way. Whatever you see or hear, be as if you hadn't seen or heard it, and judgmental evaluations won't enter your mind. When the mind does not take in externals, it is called the empty mind; when the mind does not pursue externals, it is called the peaceful mind. When the mind is peaceful and empty, the Way will naturally come to abide in it.

Once the inner mind has no attachment, external action has no artificialities. Since you are neither puritanical nor profane, praise and blame have no way to arise. Since you are neither an intellectual nor an ignoramus, profit and loss have no way to disturb you. In actual reality, you go along centered as your norm; strategically, you vary according to the times. If you can avoid getting dragged down, then you are wise in this way. If you try to control the mind too intensely, that will even cause sickness, resulting in psychological derangement.

If the mind is not agitated, then let it be; with relaxation and intensity in balance, you will always be spontaneously in tune.

If you employ thought and contrivance at the wrong time or for the wrong thing, and yet you consider yourself unattached, after all this is not genuine study. Why? The mind is like the eye: if even the finest hair gets into your eye, it is uncomfortable; if even a small matter concerns the mind, the mind will be disturbed. Once there is the affliction of disturbance, it is hard to concentrate. Therefore to practice the Way it is essential to get rid of affliction, for unless affliction is removed it is hard to attain concentration. It is like a fertile field, in which seed will not produce good crops unless the weeds are removed. Craving and cogitation are weeds of the mind; unless they are removed, concentration and wisdom will not grow.

If you extinguish all mental activity without choosing between the right and the wrong, you will cut off conscious knowing and enter into a trance of oblivion. If you let your mind act up without collecting it or governing it at all, then you'll never be different from an ordinary person. If you only cut off the sense of good and bad, so your mind has no refuge, letting ideas roam, expecting natural settling in this way, you are merely fooling yourself. If you carry out all sorts of projects claiming your mind is not influenced, this is fine talk but quite wrong in practice. Real students should especially beware of this.

Those who have the aspiration to reach the Way should conceive profound faith and devotion and cultivate practice in accord with the precepts. If you are consistent from start to finish, you will attain the true Way.

The third thing is true observation. This true observation is the way the wise attain prior awareness, the way the able practice skillful examination. Even a meal or a nap is a source of loss or gain; even a single act or a single word can be the root of disaster or fortune. Even clever maintenance of the branches is not as good as clumsy preservation of the root. Observing the root and knowing the branch is not a sense of haste either. So stop the mind, minimize concerns, and reduce contrivance. Body tranquil, mind free, you can then observe the subtle.

To cultivate the Way, the body needs food and clothing. There are some factors that cannot be neglected, some things that cannot be abandoned; accept them with an open heart, manage them with clear eyes, and do not let them impede or vex you. If you are annoyed or excited on account of things, sickness is already stirring in your mind—so what is "peace of mind"?

When there is something to strive for, don't give rise to ideas of gain and loss. Whether there is something to do or nothing to do, let the mind always be at rest. Seek as others do, but do not be covetous as others are; earn as others do, but do not hoard as others do. By not being covetous, you will be free of anxiety; by not hoarding, you will be immune to loss. Let your outward traces be like others, while your mind is always different from the vulgar. This is the model of real practice; it is essential to work on it diligently.

Even if you have severed entanglements and simplified affairs but still have afflictions that are hard to get rid of, just contemplate them methodically. For example, those most seriously afflicted by materialism or sensuality should realize that being influenced by materialism and sensuality comes from thoughts; if thoughts do not arise, there is, after all, nothing the matter. Know that thoughts of matter and sense are externally void, so the materialistic sensual mind is inwardly forgotten. When you forget thoughts, the mind is empty; who hosts matter? Scripture says, "Material forms are only ideas, and ideas are all empty—what have they to do with matter?"

If you give rise to hatred on seeing someone do wrong, that is like seeing someone try to cut his head off and then taking his knife to cut your own neck. When others do wrong on their own account, that is not your responsibility; why take on their evil and make it your own affliction? Thus when you see wrongdoers, do not hate them, and when you see people doing good, do not admire them. Why? Because both obstruct the Way.

Action is your own doing; destiny is given by Heaven. Action and destiny are to each other like echoes and shadows following sounds and forms; since they cannot be avoided, neither should they be resented. Only the wise really attain this; pleased with Heaven, knowing destiny, they therefore do not worry. How can they be made miserable by poverty or illness? Zhuangzi said, "Action enters in inescapably." Scripture says, "Heaven and earth cannot change their discipline; yin and yang cannot alter their action." This refers to true destiny—what is there to resent?

Suppose a courageous warrior encounters brigands; fearlessly he brandishes his sword and advances so that the brigands all scatter. Once the warrior's achievement is established, his honor and his pension continue to the end of his life. Now if poverty or illness trouble you, then they are brigands. If you have an upright mind, that is the courageous warrior. Intelligent contemplation is brandishing a sword. When troubles dissolve and disappear, then the battle is won. Profound calm and eternal happiness are the honor and the pension.

Whenever painful things happen to press on your mind, if you don't use this contemplation but instead develop an anxious feeling of being burdened, this is like one who encounters brigands but does nothing about them, abandoning his armor, turning his back on his troops, and running away. Incurring blame, abandoning happiness for misery—how can such a person even be pitied?

If poverty and illness pain you, contemplate this pain as deriving from having a physical self. Were there no physical self, afflictions would have nowhere to lodge.

Fourth is stable concentration. When there is no intention to concentrate and yet one is never unconcentrated, that is called stable concentration.

Control without obsession, relaxation without indulgence, no aversion in the midst of clamor, no vexation in the midst of events—this is true concentration. But one does not seek involvement in many concerns just because one is not troubled by things, and one does not take to clamor just because one is not spoiled by clamor. Freedom from obsession is the true norm; taking on tasks is for responding for happenings.

Fifth is awakening insight. Zhuangzi said, "Those who lodge in serene concentration radiate the light of Heaven." The mind is the house of the Way; when emptiness and quietude reach their climax, the Way lodges there, and insight is born. Insight comes from your basic essence; it is not something you have just now acquired. Because of confusion by greed and emotional attachment, however, it gets obscured and lost. By purification and softening, returning to purity and tranquillity, the original real spiritual consciousness gradually becomes clear of itself; that does not mean the insight has only now been specially produced.

Once insight has emerged, treasure it and keep it in your heart; do not allow excessive intellectualism to damage your concentration. It is not that engendering insight is hard; having insight but not exploiting it is what is hard. Since ancient times, those who forgot the concrete have been many, while those who forgot the abstract have been few. To be insightful but not exploit it is forgetting the abstract.

To be insightful but not exploit it makes for freedom from excesses on the Way, so one attains profound realization of true eternity. To be insightful but not exploit it, furthermore, is an artful means of enhancing stability and insight. Just enter into concentration to awaken insight; whether it happens sooner or later is not up to the individual, so do not hastily seek insight in concentration. If you seek insight, that will compromise concentration; if concentration is compromised, then there is no insight. When insight occurs without your seeking insight, this is genuine insight.

Insight enables you to know the Way; it is not attainment of the Way. Zhuangzi said, "In ancient times those who knew the Way nurtured intelligence by means of serenity; their intelligence developed, but they did not exploit it." This is called using intelligence to nurture serenity. Intelligence and serenity nurture each other, and harmony and reason emerge. Serenity and intelligence are stability and insight; harmony and reason are the Way and virtue. Intelligence without exploitation, resting in that serenity, when accumulated over a long time naturally turns into the Way and its virtue.

Sixth is attaining the Way. When there are precious minerals in a mountain, the plants and trees do not wither; when someone embosoms the Way, the physical body is permanently stabilized. By long-term cultivation, you transform the physical to be like the spiritual; refining the spirit to enter into the subtle, you unite with the Way. Then your intelligence shines boundlessly while your body is transcendent, without limit; you use the totality of matter and emptiness to function; you embody creativity to accomplish your work. True responsiveness has no set convention; your heart is on the Way and its virtues. The Way has profound power that gradually changes the body and the spirit. When the body conforms to the Way and thus merges with the spiritual, then one is called a spiritual person. With the spiritual nature open and fluid, the body does not deteriorate; because the physical being has assimilated to the Way, there is no birth or death. In concealment, the physical is assimilated to the spiritual; in manifestation, spirit is the same as energy. This is how you walk over water and fire without harm, cast no shadow in sunlight or moonlight, remain unruffled even if thunder shatters a mountain, feel unafraid even if bare swords clash right before you, view fame and profit as a flash in the pan, recognize birth and death as morbid. It is up to you whether you remain or pass away; you go in and out where there is no room. Even though your body is polluted matter, you still reach emptiness and sublimity; is not spiritual intelligence even deeper and vaster? The *Scripture on Quickening the Spirit* says, "When body and spirit are unified, that is the real body." The *Scripture on the Western Ascent* says, "By uniting body and spirit, one can last long."

The Way of absolute nonresistance has power that may be shallow or deep. When it is deep, its effect includes the physical body; when shallow, it only extends to the mind. Those whose bodies are affected are spiritual people. Those whose minds are affected only attain insight and awakening; their bodies do not escape perishing. Why? Because insight is a function of mind: use it too much and the mind is wearied. When you first attain a little insight, you get excited and talk a lot, so spiritual energy leaks out, and there is no spiritual light to bathe and nourish the body. This eventually brings about an early end; that is what scripture calls "liberation from the corpse." Therefore great people keep their illumination hidden, concealing their brilliance for the purpose of completeness; stabilizing the spirit and treasuring energy, they learn the Way and lose their willfulness. When spirit merges with the Way, that is called attaining the Way.

The body and mind of a person who has attained the Way have five times and seven signs. The five times of mind are: (1) more movement than stillness; (2) equal movement and stillness; (3) more stillness than movement; (4) stillness when there is nothing to do, returning to movement when things impinge; (5) the mind merging with the Way and no longer stirring even when impinged upon. Only when the mind reaches this last point is one at ease; the filth of wrongdoing disappears, and there are no more afflictions.

The seven bodily signs are: (1) actions are timely and the countenance is mild and pleasant; (2) chronic ailments disappear, and body and mind are light and fresh; (3) unnatural deterioration is remedied, restoring life to its original state; (4) life is extended thousands of years—such are called immortals; (5) the physical body is refined into energy—such are called real people; (6) energy is refined into a physical form—such are called spiritual people; (7) the spirit is refined to merge with the Way—such are called people who have arrived.

Even if you have studied concentration for a long time, if your mind and body do not have these five times and seven signs, you are shortening your years and polluting your constitution; when matter disintegrates, you return to the void. Under these conditions, it is not true to say of yourself that you have insight and awakening and have attained the Way. This can be declared mistaken.

Panshan's record of sayings notes, "Practitioners should establish a determined resolve and diligently refine the mind hour to hour, moment to moment, without anticipating the future. Do not harbor ambition to prevail and hope to attain transcendent freedom in that state."

Practitioners should view this body as like an ox being led to slaughter, every step bringing it closer to death. Thus death is what is on your mind; everything is cast off. Even when the things in your environment surround you with confusion, your eyes do not see any thing, your ears do not hear any thing. Forgetting every thing moment to moment, relinquishing even the body to say nothing of the rest, by refining the mind in this way, you will see results rapidly.

Practitioners keep their minds on the Way in the midst of activity as well as in quietude, in all situations, whether walking, standing still, sitting, or reclining. Unchanged by encounters with demons, unmoved when beleaguered, you are just so when at ease and just so when in peril too. Relinquishing this body without reservation, diligently progressing straight ahead, unafraid of life and death, you are then an individual with determination.

When you start to practice refining your mind ground, you must take your previous subjectivity, attachments, schemes, evaluations, hopes, calculations, antagonisms, and rivalries and cut right through them. Also take your previous obsessions with alcohol, sex, money, power, competition, judgment, clinging, craving, selfishness, perversity, ambition, and greed and stop each one of them. When you have no entanglements outside, then your body is light and exuberant; when you have no obsessions within, then your mind is light and exuberant. Inner and outer lightness and exuberance eventually become unadulterated and thoroughly familiar; then you must still be vigilant in keeping this intact at all times, careful of what you say, moderating food and drink, and minimizing slumber. With outside and inside assisting each other, mundane defilements are cleared away with nothing left at all; at that time your own original life, your basic spirit, spontaneously appears, able to act with autonomy. Then you are an unsurpassed Wayfarer.

Practitioners must do something about the ingrained habits and biased thoughts in their minds. Energetically refine your mind to relinquish them. Even the body must be relinquished when its limit arrives—how much more so all that is in the thoughts, which is all unreal! You must clear all that away, and then you will then have no psychological afflictions obstructing you.

Things outside the body, abstract or concrete, are not worth keeping in mind or keeping the mind on them. They come and go before our eyes like mosquitoes; when we brush them away, they speed up. If we make fierce attempts to dismiss those things that are hard to get out of our minds, that in itself is a seed of futile routine!

Twenty-four hours a day, understand your own mind ground: when thoughts arise, see if they are false or true. If they are false thoughts, then immediately extinguish them. If they are true thoughts, then apply them. Day or night, at all times, at every moment, when active or when still, shatter mental inflexibility.

When you fall into error, chase it away; chase it and

chase it until not a trace remains. Then the original source will be clear and clean.

Even the slightest error should be eliminated. Even the smallest virtue should be developed.

One cut severs all. When the one thought of true eternity continues unbroken forever, then there is no decay.

If you are coming and going all wrapped up in myriad things and myriad situations, even if you want to respond harmoniously, you must be able to be in charge of yourself and not just pursue things. It is like protecting your eyes: whenever there is any dust, you close your eyes and do not let it in. Keep yourself protected like this, and eventually you will see the effect. As long as the mind lets anything in, it is drawn by that, and you cannot be in charge of yourself.

When practitioners refine the mind and respond to events, they must first have inner autonomy and inner peace; then they will hit the mark every time when they respond to external events. Even if you are broken and crushed, just let the mind not move. As for which is first and which comes after, both are conditional—what definite substance do they have? The mind should be "dead," while the potential should be alive. Just go on responding to what is most immediately urgent, peacefully and calmly, without agitation or ignorance. This is what is called always being responsive while always being serene.

When things come up, you must see through them; when situations occur, you must respond to them.

Even though external objects are conditional, practitioners have to respond to them. If you respond without ego, your mind is essentially empty, and there is no obstruction when events come up. So emptiness does not interfere with myriad things, and myriad things do not interfere with emptiness. It is just as the myriad forms and myriad beings in the universe have their individual activities but do not interfere with each other. If you keep a self-image in mind, it will inevitably be brought to bear on anything that comes up, so there will be a reaction that cannot be gotten over in a hurry, resulting in collisions that agitate your mind. Once your mind is agitated, you cannot be at peace; even if you work hard all day, you'll just toil without accomplishing anything.

When you are in the midst of a lot of people, or when you have a job to do, be sure to guard your mind so that it cannot be influenced; always look for your own mistakes, and do not be concerned with the errors of others.

As it is said, "Firm and decisive, fiercely determined, cut right in two with a single stroke." People who would be greatly cultivated should work on the mind in this way. If you do not arouse a determined will and sharpen a resolute, decisive attitude but merely pass the days at leisure just as you are, even if you say you are practicing the Way, you cannot wake up and cannot get free. Ultimately you are wrapped up in arbitrary entanglements, drifting into emotional opinions. The wheel of birth and death continues to revolve, and the Way cannot be realized.

Scripture says, "Inwardly gazing on the mind, the mind has no such mind; outwardly viewing the physical body, the form has no such form. Observing things at large, things have no such thingness. Once these three are understood, you only see emptiness." This is the practice of dismissing being and returning to nonbeing. Usually people's minds are inwardly involved with preoccupations and random imagination, while their bodies are outwardly involved in honor and disgrace, profit and loss; and for things at large they have so much craving and attachment.

These are three conditions, but in sum if you are fixated on a single one of them, this is why the ancient wizards taught people that practice requires that one first depart from being; if you do not cling to being, it is empty of itself.

As for the saying that mind has no such mind, all random ideas, fixations on objects, and calculating scheming are illusory and unreal. They arise from illusory objectifications and disappear as illusory objectifications; when you look for any reality, none can be found. Therefore it is said that the mind has no such mind.

As for "the physical form has no such form," and "things have no such thingness," physical form and things disintegrate before long, ultimately returning to nothing. This is observant insight, or understanding; once you can understand, you will naturally be detached from illusions, so delusions and random imaginations spontaneously disappear without having to be eliminated. Because thoughts in the mind are all empty, therefore it is said one "only sees emptiness." This is a matter of transcendental knowledge, not run-of-the-mill quietism.

"Contemplating emptiness, it is also empty; there is nothing for emptiness to empty." This is said to get rid of the word *emptiness*. When you are fixated on being, you need to attain the power of emptiness; when you are able to be empty, there is just this "emptiness" in your heart. Thus this "emptiness" becomes an obstruction to your mind. How so? This is called getting addicted to the medicine, thus producing disease.

If practitioners cling fixedly to emptiness, they are the same as people who stick to existence. That is why ancient wizards also taught students to remove this "emptiness."

So scripture says that when you contemplate emptiness, it is also empty, as there is nothing for emptiness to empty.

"Since what is emptied is nothing, nothingness that is naught is also nonexistent." This now has us dismiss nothingness too. Once emptiness is gone and becomes one nothingness, there is still awareness of this nothing; this cognition of nothing is also an ailment, so it must also be forgotten.

Generally speaking, those who work on the great practice should not have any fixation at all. As soon as there is the slightest fixation, it doesn't matter whether the object of attachment is existence, emptiness, or nothingness—all become binding fetters. Therefore it is imperative to get rid of them; after that is sublime.

"Since nonexistent nothingness does not exist, there is profound calm and eternal peace." When you get to this point, there is nothing to get rid of anymore; the manifestation of pure, whole, uniform, natural reality is clear and calm, not coming out or going in. Thus it is called profound calm and eternal peace.

These sayings discourse on the work of emptiness; first penetrating by insight into the highest and most profound mystery, then bringing out the word *understanding*, which is utterly essential. The next two sections are redundant, so I make no notes.

The foregoing passages—some complex, some simple, some shallow, some deep, some analytic, some general, some proceeding from start to finish, some opening up in the middle—are all about the work of purifying and refining the mind in order to merge with the wonder of the Great Way of absolute nonresistance. If those who wish to learn will combine all this in practice, they will, I hope, not be far from the Way.

Essential sayings to assist potential

The *Classic of the Beginning of Culture* by the Keeper of the Pass says, "In those who skillfully detach from consciousness, consciousness turns into knowledge."

Zhang Ziyang's *Alchemical Directions* says, "To use things to refine the mind, there is nothing else to do but not keep things on your mind; then complete serenity is possible."

The *Discourse on Mind* by the Celestial Teacher of Emptiness and Tranquillity says, "Do not fear the arising of thoughts; just beware of tardiness in noticing. The arising of thoughts is sickness; not continuing them is medicine."

The *Secret Discourse on the Mysterious Pass* by the Master of the White Jade Moon says, "Have no mind on things and no things in mind."

Calling the Way, a collection by the Master of Eternal Spring, says, "When not a single thought leaves the heart, this is true emptiness."

The Master of the Cloudy Portals said, "At the first stage of meditation, thought becomes still. At the second stage of meditation, breath becomes still. At the third stage of meditation, the energy channels become still. At the fourth stage of meditation, there is total extinction and entry into great concentration."

Hao the Ancient said, "In quietude, refine energy; in the midst of clamor, refine the spirit."

In his record of sayings on resolving confusion, Barefoot Liu said, "You must conquer your mind on a single needle, a single blade of grass."

It is essential to forget feelings and conscious perceptions to gradually return to the Way. Perceptions are seeds of birth and death; if you keep consciousness of perceptions in mind, then you will conceive feelings about objects. If there are no objects inside you, then how can outward objects occur? If outward objects do not occur, inner objects do not emerge; so inside and outside are peaceful and quiet. When mind kills objects, you are a wizard. When objects kill mind, you are a mortal.

The *Water and Cloud Collection* by Master Tan of Eternal Reality says, "When people revolve ceaselessly in routine birth and death, it is just because they are mindful." The Master of the Mountain of Virtue said, "When minding occurs, all kinds of things occur; when minding disappears, all kinds of things disappear." If not a single thought occurs, then you shed birth and death. Therefore enlightened people cultivate their behavior, detaching from emotion, breaking down obstinacy and blunting sharpness, working to overcome and eliminate unwholesome states of mind in order to see the original face before birth.

Master Liu of Eternal Life said, "When you mentally penetrate something, you get out of its shell; when you penetrate myriad things, you get out of the shell of myriad things. Only then do you witness the Great Way of absolute nonresistance. If you cannot penetrate, and so remain in a state of inaction, that is called rigid voidness."

The commentary on the *Scripture of Purity and Serenity* by the Master of the Undefiled says, "Superior people of brilliant intelligence with intense insight let go of their whole beings, as if they had never even been born; they have no fixations at all. Then the mind source is spontaneously clear and calm, and true nature becomes manifest of itself."

Wang Chongyang's *Collection on Complete Reality* says: "There is a way to conquer the mind. If the mind is always calm and still, dark and silent, not seeing anything, neither inside nor outside, free of all thoughts and mental images, this is the settled mind, which is not to be conquered. If the mind gets excited at objects, falling all over itself looking for beginnings and ends, this is the confused mind, which ruins the virtues of the Way and undermines essence and life—it should not be indulged. Whatever you are doing, always strive to conquer perception, feeling, and cognition, realizing these are afflictions. Putting your nature in order is like tuning a stringed instrument. If the strings are too tight they will snap, while if they are too loose they will not be responsive. When tautness and relaxation are balanced, then the instrument is ready. It is also like making a sword; too much iron and it will snap, too much tin and it will bend. When iron and tin are balanced, then the sword is useful. Tuning and refining your true nature is a matter of embodying these two principles."

The *Mount Pan Record* of Wang the Cloud Dweller says, "Beware of gossiping about people and personalities, trends and fashions."

When some accomplishment gives you some sense of superiority, more accomplishment gives you more of a sense of superiority. Once you have a sense of superiority, then you have a self-image, which creates a massive obstacle. How can you attain the state of emptiness of mind? You have to increase your resolve and break yourself under all things, always taking a back seat to other people, thinking you are not as good as others in any way; then you can get rid of pride and a sense of superiority.

The experiences that may occur in stillness are of very many sorts, but all of them are productions of one's own consciousness which appear because of stillness. An ancient said, "Whatever has form is unreal." If you want to eliminate consciousness, the conscious spirit still remains, metamorphosing into apparitions that confuse the mind host. If the mind host is not disturbed, seeing is like not seeing; like space, there is nowhere to grasp. Then any apparitions spontaneously disappear, as there are no objects that can bewilder the mind, and no things that can disrupt it.

If you are tranquil and unagitated, how can bedevilment occur? These manifestations appear because mental wandering has not ended; remain essentially calm, and they will disappear of themselves.

When beginners polish and refine their minds, as they attain a state of stillness, extraordinary experiences or visions may occur. If they take these experiences seriously, they will become attached to falsehoods; if this is not eliminated, it will develop into incurable mental illness.

Some ask, "Those who study illustrative stories and read scriptures and classics say they are illumining the mind in the ancient teachings; is this true?"

People who practice cultivation basically refine themselves to enter from ordinariness into sagehood. If people who are not willing to make this their task just make a living on the sayings and writings of others, using up all their time pursuing literalist studies, what does this ultimately accomplish? When death comes calling, not a single phrase, not a single letter will prove useful.

This sole point of effective luminosity that animates the body has always been pure; what lack do you complain of? If you can understand it clearly yourself, it is a basis for transcending the ordinary and entering into sagehood. If you really believe this, work on it, and understand your own story, then why count the treasures of others anymore?

The *Assembled Essentials* says, "Always examine yourself: have false ideas and thoughts stopped? Are involvements with external objects at a minimum? Am I unmoved in contact with things? Are black and white undifferentiated? Are mental images in dreams accurate and unconfused? Is my heart at peace? In this manner you can measure the depth of your entry into the Way."

The above teachings all are methods of empty quietude, approaches to the Way. The essential mechanisms are all mentioned, without any concealment; if you practice in accord with them, you may be sure of attainment. The only thing to worry about is failure of will.

Some people complain that there is nothing to grasp, nothing to hold on to. What they don't realize is that the Way is basically without attachment, so to seek it with a grasping mind is inherently self-defeating. To enter the Way, the mind of a practitioner should be like space; if there is any clinging, that becomes an affliction. Then when you get sick of this affliction and want to get rid of it, you draw on yourself an extra burden on account of contrived effort. Therefore nothing compares to being careful of the beginning; if there is no clinging to start with, you will end up without affliction. So don't seek isolated skills or disciplines that are easy to perform just because this nonattachment is hard to manage, for if you do you will ruin yourself.

Some ask if the Great Way of absolute nonresistance can prolong life. Lao-tzu said, "What gives us life is the Way; what enlivens us is the spirit." If you can keep mindful of the spirit, even if locked in death energy, you can cause the dry bones of seven generations of ancestors to have living energy. Wen-tzu said, "The highest masters nurture the spirit; lesser ones nurture the body. When the spirit is clear and the mood equanimous, then the physical body is at peace. This is the basis of hygiene." Wen-tzu also said, "When the spirit is not focused externally, that is called spirituality; to keep the spirit intact is called integrity." Speaking on this basis, absolute nonresistance is truly the foremost principle of long life.

However, while it may be that long life comes about spontaneously if you keep the spirit intact, nevertheless if you seek long life you are fixated on long life. Lao-tzu said, "Even I am gray; who can keep intact forever?" Long Life Liu said, "How can you seek eternal life by means of a temporal body?" How fine these words are—practitioners of mysticism can thereby be free of confusion.

With the decline of the Way of wizardry, the true teaching is not flourishing, while false teachings are popular. Beginners don't know how to orient their efforts, and true guides in this quest are hard to find; the blind are leading the blind, into a pit of fire. If you withdraw and seek it in books, you find complicated ramifications, so your questions grow more and more; the true vehicle is easily obscured, while tangential methods are so abundant that they block you, ultimately leaving you with no basis for progress or detachment. At a loss, you may simply stop, or you may slight faith and act arbitrarily, destroying your body and losing your essential nature. This is very lamentable.

Now in order to sweep away worn-out cliches I open up what has not yet been opened, enabling people of later generations to realize what is mistaken and what is accurate, to understand how to get started and how to arrive at the goal. In this way I hope to revive religion somewhat and block the waves of madness.

The way of eternal life through perception of vital spirit • The bases of alchemy: The absolute, yin and yang, substance and function

Zhang Ziyang said, "The way of restorative alchemy is most simple and easy; it is like a circle." Yu Yuwu said, "What is the circle? It is the Absolute of the *Book of Changes*. When the Absolute goes into motion, it produces yin and yang. When motion culminates, it reverts to stillness and in stillness produces yin. When stillness culminates, it returns to movement. Movement and stillness in alternation constitute bases for each other. This is the wonder of Creation, the natural course of the Way."

Zhang Sanfeng said, "The absolute is the Way of nonresistance and spontaneity. The two modalities are yin and yang. The absolute is the basic spirit; the two modalities are vitality and energy. The absolute is the matrix of the alchemical elixir; the two modalities are true lead and true mercury. Symbolized by a circle, the absolute is itself infinite. This is also called the Great Transmutation, which is none other than the countenance before birth. 'Absolute unity containing true energy' is a reference to the state of the universal inception, prior to the division of the two polar energies."

Yi Zhenzi said, "The physical cannot produce the physical; what produces the physical is not physical, it is energy. What produces energy is not energy, it is the Way." He also said, "The myriad differences in the physical form change and do not remain; only the unity of energy does not change. But the unchanging energy perishes, while the cause of its unchanging remains."

Although the way of wizardry is not beyond yin and yang and the five elements, nevertheless yin and yang and the five elements cannot operate themselves without the absolute. The absolute is the unifying law of yin and yang and the five elements. If you want to operate yin and yang and the five elements in your own body, do not by any means focus your effort on yin and yang and the five elements. You must concentrate on the absolute, practicing being unborn; then yin and yang and the five elements will operate spontaneously and naturally without your having to seek to operate them. This is an unknown truth that brings out the whole matter by getting to the gist of it. If you are confused about this and work on operating yin and yang and the five elements, well, yin and yang and the five elements are not things that can be operated by human knowledge or technique. The slightest deviation in your practice can lead to a hundred bizarre changes; you may go to your death without turning back, ultimately unable to operate yin and yang and the five elements.

Alchemy takes its rules from creation

The *Classic of Invisible Correspondences* says, "Observe the course of Nature; hold to the conduct of Nature." Spiritual alchemy certainly takes its laws from Creation, but not by practicing imitation of each individual particular. The ancients were mentally meshed with Nature and acted in concert with its course, the Way. Thus does the energetic operation of the body spontaneously conform to Nature. If you seek the elixir by obsessively trying to imitate the traces of Nature with the secular attitude so commonplace today, that's not it!

Foundations of alchemy • *Furnace and cauldron*

Some ask what the furnace and cauldron are. Li Qing-an said, "Body and mind are the cauldron and furnace." An alchemical text says, "First take Heaven and Earth for the cauldron; then make a ball of yin and yang and cook it." Heaven is mind, Earth is body. People today who set up an external furnace and cauldron are mistaken.

The furnace and cauldron are the body and mind. To cultivate refinement, there has to be the body; then spirit and energy have a base and do not disperse, and the work has a basis on which to be carried out. This is what is called borrowing the temporal to cultivate the real. Since the furnace and cauldron are the means by which substances can be cooked and transmuted, the Master of the Pass used the term *pot*, which was later changed to furnace and cauldron. Using this symbolism for the body can be considered clever and apropos. There are many different terms, such as the inner furnace and outer furnace mentioned in the *Triplex Unity*, but their essential meaning does not go beyond this. Yu Yuwu said, "In spiritual alchemy, the cosmic void is the furnace and cauldron; in the cosmic void there is a natural subtle function, spontaneously occurring." This cosmic void has no self, no person, no inside, no outside: how can furnace and cauldron express it? Yuwu is just using a simile to make his point; that is not his underlying meaning.

A point falls into the yellow court

The *Book of Balance and Harmony* says, "After mating in the chamber of Heaven, a point falls into the Yellow Court."

When the point falls into the Yellow Court, where does it wind up? What people don't realize is that practitioners should just mate spirit and energy. There is no need to ask where the result winds up, because it settles in its place naturally. Medical texts describe the processes of digestion, absorption, and elimination as occurring naturally, without people having to arrange them. Similarly, the true energy in the body rises and descends, starting from the source and returning to the source, naturally having its own place of abode; what need is there for people to visualize it in order to arrange it?

Alchemical ingredients • *Basic energy is where the body is born*

The *Triplex Unity* says, "The body a human receives is originally a nothingness; basic vitality circulates, getting a start from energy."

While it is true that human birth comes from the combination of sperm and ovum, nevertheless what makes birth possible is the energy of the basic harmony of heaven and earth. Without this energy, even if there are sperm and ovum they cannot make a being. So evidently the true energy of basic harmony is the root of the physical, the place where the body is born. As people receive this energy while yet unborn, it can produce being out of nonbeing, causing the body to grow and develop. So if you cultivate this basic energy today, why couldn't you prolong life, see eternity, escape constriction, and become spiritually transformed?

Basic vitality

The Master Embracing Unity said, "The firing and harmonizing of absolute unity cultivating gold alchemical elixir refines just two things: vitality and soul."

The Master of Silent Sunlight said, "Why must cultivation need yellow sprouts for roots? The basic energy in the human body arises daily; it is just because of not knowing how to preserve and nurture it that it is invaded and stripped away by two distortions. What two distortions? Environmental extremes are distorters of energy; emotional extremes are distorters of sense. These two distortions are robbers of basic energy, attacking it day and night; thus basic energy is thinned and weakened, even to the point of morbidity. Ancient wizards knew that preservation of life is a matter of keeping basic energy stable. Nevertheless, it fluctuates easily. Why? Only basic vitality can keep it stable. That is why it is an established method of cultivation to teach people to make basic vitality rise to preserve basic energy, combining them in one place, completely stable and steadfast, not worn out or scattered. If you can ward off the attacks of the two distortions, only then can you prolong life, see forever, and not die!

Zhang Ziyang said, "When vitality fills you within and energy melts it, it rises with energy to constitute true lead."

The statements by the first two wizards indicate the reason practical alchemy uses basic vitality; the last statement indicates the function of basic vitality.

Basic vitality is sexual vitality

Zhang Ziyang said, "Using vitality, use basic vitality; this is not sexual vitality."

Basic vitality and sexual vitality are fundamentally not two things. When someone is not feeling sexuality, there is no location in the body where vitality is. Medical literature says that the genitals are the seat of vitality; it also says that each of the internal organs has stored vitality. In reality, there is no vitality abiding in specific places. Vitality merges into basic energy, without taking on form or substantiality; only practitioners of the Way can concentrate the basic energy and distill the vitality. Because this vitality arises spontaneously with sexual feeling, it is called basic vitality. Ordinary people do not know how to distill it and cannot extract the vitality for practical use, so the basic vitality cannot develop. In sexual intercourse, basic energy changes into vitality, which descends from the brain down the spine and out the urethra; this semen is a material substance, representing the vitality of sexuality. When it arises in true unity, it is basic vitality; when it leaks out during sexual intercourse, it is sexual vitality. As transmutations of basic energy, basic vitality and sexual vitality are one; it is a mistake to split them into two.

Basic energy produces basic vitality

Master Ziyang said, "When basic energy is born, basic vitality is produced."

Hu Huncheng said, "Collect primal generative energy for medicine." This primal energy of true unity is undifferentiated within abstract ecstasy; wizards take this energy and refine it into an elixir, calling this the seed of realization. The energy of absolute unity containing reality is the undifferentiated energy prior to the division of heaven and earth. It is the communion of basic energy in the body. After basic energy is born, basic vitality is produced; this is the arising of initial positive energy in the body. Vitality and energy are one thing; when we speak of energy, vitality is included. This is why it is said that energy is life-increasing medicine.

Detachment from emotional consciousness to nurture basic harmony

Yu Yuwu said, "The science of spiritual alchemy is all a matter of the uniform energy of basic harmony, from which a wealth of transformations evolve."

Master Ziyang said, "To preserve basic harmony, nothing takes precedence over detachment from emotional consciousness."

The reason things sprout in spring and not in summer, fall, or winter is because of harmony. When people are free from emotional consciousness, then their energy is harmonious. When energy is harmonious, it mellows and expands, and the harmony of heaven and earth also responds to it. Would it not then be possible to extend life?

Nowadays people's desires and emotions get excited in the midst of daily activities, so the action of their energy is flighty, unstable, suffocated, and depressed. It is as if the weather were suddenly cold and then suddenly hot, scorching in winter and frosty in summer—is this basic harmony? Since it is inharmonious, there is the possibility of aberration and illness, destructive to life—how then could one hope for longevity, eternal vision, and attainment of the Way? So it is said that to preserve basic harmony, nothing takes precedence over detachment from emotional consciousness.

Alchemy requires interruption of craving

The *Mystic Mirror of the Great Leader* says, "Pure yang rising is called energy; pure yin descending is called fluid. Energy and fluid combined in the bones and vessels is called marrow. Energy and marrow combined in the prostate is called semen. When heart energy is in the liver but the vitality of the liver is infirm, then the eyes are dim. When heart energy is in the lungs but the vitality of the lungs is not full, the flesh is thin and weak. When heart energy is in the kidneys and genitals but the vitality of the kidneys and genitals is infirm, the energy of the spirit is diminished. When heart energy is in the spleen but the vitality of the spleen is infirm, the teeth and hair loosen and fall out. Among the vital organs, the genitals are the pivot of vitality, while the heart is the office of energy. When true vitality is in the genitals, the other vitalities spontaneously return to the lower field; when true energy is in the heart, the other energies naturally return to the capital."

The *Simpleton* says, "When water has a source, the flow will be long; when a tree has a root, its foliage will be luxuriant. When a house has a foundation, its pillars will be upright; when people have vitality, their lives will be long."

The *Classic of the Yellow Court* says, "To prolong life, beware of haste in the bedroom; excessive intensity inevitably makes the spirit weep." It also says, "Give up debauched lust, and focus on preserving vitality; then you can live with but little land and a modest house."

Master Ziyang said, "When vitality is lost and basic energy does not arise, then original positivity does not appear."

Practical wizardry is a mater of stabilizing vitality; then the root is strong and living energy flourishes daily. If a lustful attitude is not stopped, spiritual roots will not be firm; then the accumulation of vitality thins daily, and the production of basic energy lessens daily. Gradually you reach exhaustion and even death. Chan Buddhists say in this regard, "If you study meditation and contemplation without interrupting craving, that is like steaming sand to make rice—no matter how long you may steam it, you'll never get anything but hot sand, not rice." So if you want to build up basic energy, first you should stop debauchery and lustfulness; this work must be done with a clean mind free from thoughts. Worldly people ignorant of this use physical pressure to stop the emission of semen in sexual intercourse, thinking that to be prevention of leakage. They do not know that vitality is to be stabilized before it has created a concrete substance. If you wait till it has made substance and then try to stop it, the semen may not be emitted but the spiritual energy is long gone. How ignorant it is to keep deteriorating, stagnant matter accumulating in the pelvic region, thus producing bizarre ailments! Even more in error are blind teachers who go on to fool people by saying they should draw their semen up their spine, calling this "restoration of vitality to repair the brain."

Basic spirit using medicine

Some ask which is most important—vitality, energy, or spirit. Master Ziyang said, "Spirit is most important."

The basic spirit is the true mind, which is the true essence. The medicine used therefore is not material medicine; the subtle action of the work of wizardry is all in this essence. Ancient custom listed it as a medicine, but later Taoists ignorant of the root source of the Great Way often disregarded this. So basic spirit wound up as a "medicine," with an extra "intent" outside the basic spirit to employ it. Nothing could be more incoherent than this. It is no wonder people don't attain wizardry!

The basic spirit is the thinking spirit

Master Ziyang said, "Using spirit, use the basic spirit, not the thinking spirit."

He also said, "What is the basic spirit? Once the absolute has divided, we are imbued with this point of living light, which is basic essence. Basic essence is nothing other than energy that is congealed and alive." And, "When the basic spirit appears, the basic energy arises; when basic essence is restored, basic energy is born."

Some ask if the basic spirit and the thinking spirit are one or two. Mind, essence, and spirit are one: it is called basic spirit by virtue of being imbued with the point of living luminescence from Heaven. When this basic spirit is later moved by emotional consciousness, the basic spirit sinks into emotional consciousness and turns into the thinking spirit. In reality, even though thought has emotional consciousness, the basic spirit is always complete and whole, neither defective nor lacking. If people can turn their attention back to this and detach from their emotional consciousness, then the thinking is none other than a subtle function of the basic spirit!

The opening of the mysterious pass

L i Qing-an said, "As for the opening of the mysterious pass, wherever material elements or physical forces adhere is not it, and yet it cannot be sought outside the body."

He also said, "Just seek inwardly twenty-four hours a day, in the midst of all activities: what is it that speaks and keeps silent, that sees and hears?"

He also said, "The ancients just wrote the word *center* as an indication for people. This word *center* is the opening of the mysterious pass. The center does not mean inside as opposed to outside, nor does it mean the center as opposed to the four directions, nor does it mean the center as the middle. Buddhists say that when you don't think good or bad this is your original face. Taoists say this is where thoughts do not arise."

Chen the Blank said, "It takes no more than the method of turning the light around and looking inward, cleaning up thoughts."

The Master of the Jade Valley Stream said, "The central issue is having an upright mind and sincere intention."

This indicates that the basic spirit is the opening of the mysterious pass.

Chen the Nirvanic said, "Just sit quietly in stable concentration with no thoughts in thoughts. When this work is pure, you become unified, silent all day, like a hen sitting on her eggs. Then you naturally see the opening of the mysterious pass, so vast there is no outside, yet so minute there is no inside. From this you cull primal whole energy, which constitutes the matrix of the alchemical elixir. Practice diligently, and you will be able to ride with the wizards of old."

Master Ziyang said, "This opening has no borders or

edges, no inside or outside; it is the root of spiritual energy, the valley of absolute nonresistance."

This indicates that absolute nonresistance is the opening of the mysterious pass. When you are absolutely empty and utterly still, there is no more self; you only feel a mystic merging with the universe, with spiritual energy fermenting therein. This is the finest state of cultivation, so it is called the opening of the mysterious pass.

The handle of alchemy

The *Classic of Hidden Correspondences* says, "The North Star is the mainspring of the sky; the mind is the mainspring of the human being."

The *Treatise on Gold Liquid Restorative Elixir* says, "The river source where the medicine is produced, the subtle directions for extraction and addition in the firing process, and even the incubation and completion of the elixir are not apart from the function of the mind."

Master Ziyang's *Alchemical Directions* says, "The reason mind is considered wondrous is that energy comes from its opening, while vitality follows its call. Since energy comes from its opening, when the mind is harmonious the energy is harmonious, and when the energy is harmonious the body is harmonious. When the body is harmonious, the harmony of heaven and earth responds. So when emotions are strong and thus energy is inharmonious, it is because emotions arise in the mind. As for vitality following its call, when men and women have sexual intercourse and their vitality flows, it is also the mind that causes it. When the mind is pure, thoughts are pure; when thoughts are pure, vitality is born."

Master Tan of the Purple Corona said, "Spirit is like the

mother; energy is like the child. Summoning energy by spirit is like a mother calling her child, who is sure to come."

Mind is certainly the handle of wizardry. Even though everyone has mind, however, not everyone attains wizardry. This is not the fault of mind itself but the fault of the mind lingering on desires and thus being unable to be quiet and empty.

Barefoot Liu said, "Spirit and energy have a natural affinity, like child and mother, but as long as they are separated by mundane feelings, they cannot meet. If you lessen mundane feelings a bit, to that extent circulation will take place."

Yu Yuwu said, "When mind is steady, spirit is stable and energy is harmonious; there is natural circulation up and down through the three chambers, and the hundred channels naturally flow freely."

Li Qing-an said, "Mind returns to empty silence, the body enters nondoing, and inside and outside are forgotten; at this point, vitality naturally changes into energy, energy naturally changes into spirit, and spirit naturally returns to emptiness."

Li Qing-an also said, "When body and mind are both quiet, Heaven and Earth merge; in real potential's subtle response, naturally occurring, an extraordinary movement takes place. In this movement is where the 'heart of heaven' is seen: the medicine, furnace, and cauldron are herein; the various functions of the three bases, eight trigrams, four forms, and five elements are all in this."

Speaking from this point of view, if the mind is not quiet and empty, then it fails to do its job; even with vitality and energy there, it cannot make use of them. Why do people today speak only of refining lead and mercury and not of mastering mind?

Alchemical operations • *The mysterious female*

L i Qing-an said, "The mysterious female is the mechanism of the closing and opening of heaven and earth. The *I Ching* says, 'Closing the door is called earth, opening the door is called heaven.' Cyclic closing and opening represent cyclic movement and quiescence. This is what Lao-tzu meant by 'using it without force.' "

Li Qing-an also said, "Master Ziyang said that the mysterious female is the place where thoughts arise. This is correct. I say that the place where thoughts arise is the root of birth and death—is this not the mysterious female?"

Lao-tzu said, "The open spirit not stagnating is called the mysterious female." *Open* means empty; the open spirit refers to taking care of the spirit so that it is empty, unoccupied, and open. *Mysterious* means subtle. *Female* refers to the fact that emptiness is where things are born. The open spirit is the mysterious female. Limitless subtle functions are born from within the open spirit; this is the opening of the mysterious female. This is the orthodox explanation; next is Li Qing-an's twofold explanation. Later generations singled out a specific place in the body as the mysterious female and claimed that the open spirit is based on the mysterious female. But if the open spirit were based on the mysterious female, that would mean it would have adherence; then it could not be open spirit. There are also later expositors of the mysterious female who explain it in dozens of ways, adding more and more confusion and error!

The bellows

The *Tao Te Ching* says, "The space between heaven and earth is like a bellows, empty and uninhibited, producing more and more with movement."

The *Treatise on the Rise and Descent of Yin and Yang* says, "If people can emulate the rising and falling bellows action of heaven and earth, breath going out when opening, breath going in when closing, the going out like the energy of earth rising, the going in like the energy of heaven descending, rising and descending alternately, then you can equal the perpetuity of heaven and earth."

The *Tao Te Ching* speaks of the bellows simply as a simile for subtle function in emptiness; when later generations borrowed it to express the mechanism of rising and descending, this was a good idea too.

Nowadays when Taoists speak of pumping the bellows, they do not mean pumping a bellows; they mean tuning true breathing. If you know the furnace and cauldron but not the bellows, then yin and yang are separated; even though furnace and cauldron be set up, they are useless. If you know how to pump a bellows but not how to tune true breathing, then you're missing the essential subtlety whereby the pumping is done. How will you snatch the wholesome energy of heaven and earth to crystallize the elixir?

Sixty hexagrams symbolizing the alchemical firing process

The *Triplex Unity* says, "In the mornings, [the *I Ching* hexagram] Difficulty deals with things; in the evenings [the hexagram] Darkness should be accepted. Use a hexagram for each day and night, according to the order, up to Settled and Unsettled, reaching the dawn twilight; when you come to the end, you start again."

Originally the lines of the *I Ching* hexagrams were just used in opposite pairs to correspond to the rise and descent of the alchemical process. The two hexagrams Difficulty and Darkness, for example, are opposites. In terms of the structure of the Difficulty hexagram, from the first line up to the top line is like yang fire, the "fire" of positive energy, rising from below up to the crown. Seen upside down, as if starting from the top line of Difficulty, it becomes the hexagram Darkness; this is like the yin convergence, or passive union, descending from above to the Yellow Court in the center. The pair is just one hexagram, seen upright and upside down. This is like the alchemical firing process; it is basically only one "fire" or energy, but there is rise and descent.

The other hexagrams are also like this, consisting of eight complements that can also be seen oppositely. If you comprehend this, then the mechanism of the firing process is in yourself, and you can do without the hexagram lines.

Symbolizing the firing process by the year, month, and day, humanity and duty, joy and anger, reward and punishment

The *Triplex Unity* says, "Spring and summer, rest on inner substance, from the Rat to the Dragon and Snake; fall and winter are appropriate for external action, from the Horse to the Dog and Boar. Reward and punishment correspond to spring and autumn; darkness and light conform to cold and heat. The words of the *I Ching* lines contain humanity and duty; anger and joy occur according to the time."

Ancient wizards used the opposite pairs in the sixty hexagrams of the *I Ching* to symbolize the rise and descent of one energy; this can be considered brilliant, but it did not cover the matter of waxing and waning, so they talked about this in terms of the seasons of a year and the waxing and waning of the moon in a lunar cycle. Everyone can see the waxing and waning of the moon in the sky, so using this to observe the functions of waxing and waning of yin and yang in our bodies is indeed clear and easy to understand. Nevertheless, the mechanisms of movement and stillness are still not thoroughly comprehended in this manner, so people use the time of day to express them. Generally speaking, the times from the hour of the Tiger (3:00–5:00 A.M.) to the hour of the Dog (7:00–9:00 P.M.) are active, while the hours of the Boar (9:00–11:00 P.M.), the Rat (11:00 P.M.–1:00 A.M.), and the Ox (1:00–3:00 A.M.) are still. This is all there is to it, but it is imperative to know measure, to avoid excess and insufficiency, so there are also expressions using the terms humanity and duty, joy and anger, and reward and punishment. Ancient wizards drew on symbols and exemplifications, so layers upon layers of perception emerge, but in the final analysis there is not a single excessive word. These should be understood by practitioners—why overlook them just because they are symbolic?

Intent as the go-between

M aster Ziyang said, "Is intent only the go-between? The science of spiritual alchemy can never be apart from it, from beginning to end."

The Master of Round Unity said, "The reason practical wizardry needs intent is essentially just to assess the operation and keep it in balance. Intent is associated with the spleen; that is why wizards call it true earth. True earth means harmony. Now in medical practice, a pulse may be floating or sinking, slow or rapid, empty or full, but as long as there is stomach energy, one does not die. So the stomach energy is also harmony.

"In spiritual alchemy, active and quiet exercises must not be off balance in the slightest; if there is any imbalance, it usually results in illness. Throughout it is essential to assess relative gravity, relative buoyancy, relative strength, and relative freshness and to adjust them, causing yin and yang to match each other, so water and fire are evenly balanced, not allowing excess, which would cause other troubles. If not for intent operating this assessment, how could you guarantee you won't make a mistake and go wrong?"

Zhang Sanfeng said, "What is intent? It is the outward function of the basic spirit; it is not that there is also intent in addition to the basic spirit."

Master Ziyang said, "Mind is the natural leader: when it is used without artificiality, then what activates it is the basic spirit. This is the alchemical use of mind."

So you should not overactivate intent. Once you overactivate intent, you are trying to force progress and not being natural. The problems caused by the toil of forced exercises are not trivial; even if you use them skillfully, you still do not escape attachment, contrarily increasing the ailment of intention. This is why votaries of the Sect of Life do not reach the Great Way of absolute nonresistance.

The location of the awareness of the basic spirit is intent; awareness without an effort to be conscious is skillful use of intent. If you have even a single thought of deliberate arrangement, then you are overactivating intent.

The way of seeing vital spirit and perpetuating life • Alchemical tasks • Stabilizing the furnace and setting up the cauldron

In *Precious Writings of the Nine Realized Ones,* the Master of Pure Sunlight said, "Those who would cultivate alchemy first make the furnace upright. The furnace surrounds the cauldron; it is the body. The furnace is divided into eight faces, namely the ears, eyes, mouth, nose, form, color, nourishment, and taste. These are the openings of the bellows: one should always guard them, not letting the eight influences of wind and cold, heat and humidity, hunger and fullness, and fatigue and ease damage them externally and not letting the six brigands of hatred, craving, ebullience, anger, sorrow, and indulgence damage them internally."

The True Lord of the Undifferentiated Origin said, "If those who cultivate their bodies always have their basic energy broken, then their vital spirit cannot be whole. It is necessary for the vital spirit to be complete and the energy whole before it is possible to develop life to become an immortal."

Beginning learners should first understand the stabilization of the furnace and setting up of the cauldron: be careful of your activities, moderate consumption, regulate temperature, minimize slumber, collect body and mind, be sparing of vitality, be sparing of energy, be sparing of spirit; make the body peaceful, the spirit complete, and the energy strong, and then this body and mind can be the furnace and cauldron into which medicine can be put. Without this preparatory work, the furnace and cauldron will break and leak and will not be suitable for use; if you try to put medicine in there, you will have trouble. Yu Yuwu had a saying, "If you have medicine and carry out the firing process, then metal will be pressured by fire to leap up to the heart chamber, where it turns to water and then subdues the fire so that there is no problematic overheating. If you carry out the firing process without medicine, then empty yang will rise aggressively; you will only burn your body."

First, prepare a quiet room.

The quiet room does not have to be in the mountains or the woods. It may be in the city or in the provinces. As long as you have a place that's useful for the purpose, it doesn't matter where it is. The room should not be too bright, for that would hurt the yang soul, and it should not be too dark, for that would hurt the yin soul. There should be no objects in the room but an incense burner and a bench.

Second, develop will.

In this endeavor, unless you concentrate on developing your will on account of birth and death, you are highly likely to give up along the way. Therefore you must have unbending determination, persistent thought, and unflagging energy; first let go of yourself, then let go of your holdings, and be unfazed by sickness or even death. Only then have you any hope of success.

Alchemy doesn't work if you are inconsistent. If you work on it when you are in the mood, but then get distracted by things and slack off when this mood wanes, then your spirit is influenced and your energy taken away when you are not practicing, just like someone with no accomplishment at all. Even if you get into the mood to work again, it will be like lacing with too many missing strings—it won't be effective at all.

What you must do is bury your past: cut off the time that has already gone by and don't ask about it. Just rouse your vigor from this moment on, working consistently with all your effort whether or not there is anything to deal with, whether the situation is pleasing or displeasing: a day like an hour, a year like a day, a millennium like a year. Then there is no day or night, no noon or midnight, no dawn or dusk, no end or beginning of the lunar cycle, no partiality or completeness, no opening or closing; you do not hope to ascend to wizardhood and do not set up a limit, except for this whole lifetime. Only thus do you gain a little bit of accord.

Third, set aside involvements.

Taoist study cannot have any externals burdening the mind. If you are preoccupied with family affairs, political or professional affairs, social intercourse, charms and spells, curing and divining, literature, riding, music, martial arts, gambling, or handicrafts, all of this will inhibit your mind and confuse your essential nature, so you should be very wary of it.

Fourth, practice sitting.

When you sit, spread sitting mats thickly to prevent physical discomfort and pain. Loosen your clothing and belt to prevent stagnation of energy.

To sit in the lotus posture, first put the left foot on the right thigh, then put the right foot on the left thigh. In the half lotus posture, the left foot is on the right foot. Either way will do. Next, put the left hand in the right palm, such that the thumb tips are propped up against each other. Slowly lift your body up and move from side to side to achieve a proper balance of relaxation and tension. Then sit up straight, such that your waist, spine, and neckbones support each other, ears aligned with shoulders, nose aligned with navel, the tongue against the upper palate, lips and teeth touching. The eyes should be slightly open; they should not be completely shut, for this is the "ghost cave in the mountain of darkness," where it is extremely easy to become oblivious and unseeing, and it is also possible to become possessed.

The body should be straight, like Buddha, not leaning to the left or right, not tilting forward or backward. Don't lean against a support, lest you become lazy. Sitting should be relaxed and natural. The shoulders should not be too erect, for if they are too erect it is hard to persevere. Practice should not be too intense, for if too intense it will be easily interrupted. The essential thing is to find the mean.

The breath should pass through the nose. Respiration should not be coarse, should not be forced, should not be suppressed, and should not be stopped. Inhalation and exhalation should be smooth and gentle, but you should not fix your attention on this.

Once your physical posture is steady and your breathing is tuned, relax your abdomen and do not think of good or bad at all. When a thought arises, notice it; once you become aware of it, it is not there. Eventually you forget mental objects and spontaneously become unified. If you get this, you will naturally feel light and fresh; this is what is called the method of comfort.

For those who have already awakened, this is like a dragon

finding water; for those who have not, just develop your will, and you will not be cheated.

When you come out of concentration, move your body slowly and get up calmly and carefully. Preserve the power of concentration at all times, like taking care of a baby, and the power of concentration will be easy to perfect. As it is said, to search for a pearl it's better if the water is calm; if the water is agitated, it will be hard to find. When the water of concentration is calm and clear, the pearl of mind appears of itself.

The river source where medicine is produced

The *Triplex Unity* says, "Metal is the mother of water; the mother conceals the fetus of the child. Mercury is the child of metal; the child is hidden in the womb of the mother."

Yu Yuwu said, "Water is the root source of the great elixir. Heaven produces water, its place in the north, represented by the water trigram; this is where the medicine in our bodies is produced. Alchemy is based on water; metal vitality is produced in water."

This refers to basic vitality being produced in the genitals. Yuan the Absolutist said, "Wizards borrow the genital region for the ground of production; this is not using the genitals, but though one does not use the genitals, nevertheless practical exercise is done within the genitals." That is why the genitals are considered the "river source where the medicine is produced."

Some people, not knowing the meaning of this, simply hear that wizardry does not use the heart and genitals and then seek outside the genitals. They say the central aperture between the genitals and kidneys is where true yang lies hidden, and that alchemical praxis simply uses fire to press this true yang out to function. But if true yang is hidden in an aperture, how is that different from being hidden in the genitals? And how does using an aperture differ from using the genitals? The major teaching of wizardry regards everything in the ordinary body as temporal residue and does not use it. If there were actually basic energy lying concealed inside an aperture, it too would be a temporal residue. These are biased views unworthy of discussion.

The receptive is the abode of the way

The *Triplex Unity* says, "The Receptive is calm and collected; it is the abode of the Way."

This refers to how basic vitality is produced. Although basic vitality is produced in the genitals, nevertheless it is impossible to produce it without being calm and collected. The yang energy of a year is born in Return, based on The Receptive. The moonlight of a month is reborn at the beginning of the lunar cycle, based on the end of the lunar cycle. The yang energy of a day is born in the midnight hour, based on the late night hour. These are the same as our basic vitality being produced in collected calmness. All these energies arise from collection, so the great elixir has its abode in The Receptive.

Yang disburses, yin receives

The *Triplex Unity* says, "Male yang disburses, dissemi-
nating mystery; female yin transmutes, encircling the
center."

It also says, "Yang endows, yin receives; female and male
need each other."

These are general expressions of the principle of disbursing
and receptivity of yin and yang in heaven and earth and all
things.

It also says, "Constancy and accord are patterns of earth,
accepting the disbursement of heaven."

This refers to The Creative disbursing energy to The Receptive and The Receptive accepting it accordingly.

It also says, "The sun gives power; the moon thereby gives
light."

This refers to the sun giving light to the moon.

It also says, "The mother takes in rich liquid, which the
father gives."

This refers to the father giving energy to the mother.

This is precisely where basic energy is produced. Basic vitality arises from being calm and collected, to be sure, but if
the heart energy does not descend to mix with the genitals,
and the genitals receive nothing, how can it collect produc-
tively?

Filling cosmic space is one basic energy alone: this energy
is heaven, while the great mass formed of the residue in this
energy is earth. The waning and waxing of this energy are yin
and yang.

Every year in autumn and winter this energy withdraws
into the earth. Then at the solstice it starts to rise again. As it
keeps on being produced and developing, it accumulates and

gradually rises. When it reaches its peak, then it gradually wanes again. This is the way it has been throughout time.

This energy is what causes plants to sprout from the earth; without this energy, the earth cannot produce anything. So that which produces things is earth, while that whereby things are produced is the energy of heaven. It is just a matter of being able to collect and disburse it. Similarly, in alchemy, it is necessary for the heart energy to descend and mix with the genitals and the genitals to receive and collect it before it is possible to produce transformation.

Congealing spirit in the energy aperture

Verses on Restoring Life says, "The sun moves into the moonlight."

The Master of the White Jade Moon said, "All you need to do is congeal spirit in the energy aperture."

These sayings refer to the descent of heart energy into intercourse. This is called chasing the dragon to the tiger or putting mercury into lead. Congealment does not mean solidification: spirit is most ethereal, most subtle, able to fly into the heavens and plunge into the earth—how could it be solidified? So-called congealing of spirit means stopping thoughts and returning spirit to the heart so that it does not run outside; then energy also returns to the body, gradually sinking into the energy aperture.

Some ask if the energy aperture really has an opening or not and just where this aperture is. Hu the Whole said it is between the kidneys and the genitals. The Preserver of Truth said, "Once people are born, the true energy of basic positivity is dispersed throughout the body, potentiating perception, speech, and activity; how could there by any logic to considering it confined within one aperture?" If this aperture really existed, it would be more important than the internal organs—so why is it not listed in medical classics and anatomical charts? Why don't people lacking in basic energy take medicine to treat this aperture?

The fast is that those on a small path, a sidetrack, mistakenly indicate a particular place in the body and have people concentrate mentally on this place, calling that congealing the spirit in the energy aperture. Among people who follow this without understanding, there are always those who make themselves ill. This is how "congealing the spirit in the energy aperture" causes people to go wrong.

So what is the energy aperture? It is the flower pond. What is the flower pond? The Master of True Sunlight said, "The flower pond is in the ocean of energy." If you cling to the word *aperture* or *opening*, you will try to find a corresponding opening inside the body; then if we call it the flower pond, you will seek a pond inside the body, and if we call it an ocean, you will seek an ocean in the body. Will that do?

Essentially, alchemy borrows the genitals as the ground of production. This is metaphorically called the ocean of energy because it is a pool of energy; it is metaphorically called the energy aperture because it is deep and located below. It is metaphorically called the flower pond because it is where the golden efflorescence arises. That's all there is to these terms. To make the elixir, all that is required is that energy sink into this place. That is why it is called congealing spirit in the energy aperture; it does not mean deliberate focus of concentration there! The Master of Eternal Spring said, "When it is present somewhere, then it is absent somewhere; when it is not in a particular place, then there is nowhere it is not."

Alchemy produces being from nothingness. If you fail to seek the mechanism in nothingness and instead create ramifications of being, is that not a mistake?

Turning the light around to illumine inwardly

M aster Yuan of the Cosmic Void said, "The method of congealing the spirit in the energy aperture is simply a matter of gathering in your seeing, reversing your listening, and turning around the light to illumine the inward."

Master Cai's *Alchemical Guide* says, "Spirit in a human being is like fire in wood: if the fire does not come out, the wood remains; if the spirit does not go out, the body survives. When fire gives off light outwardly, the fuel is being used up; when the spirit's intellect is racing outwardly, wholeness is disintegrating."

Yu Yuwu said, "Spiritual wizards' method of cultivation has people turn their light around to illumine the inward, breathing universal harmony. This is all about return to the root source, going back to the beginning where energy is received at birth."

Turning the light around to illumine inwardly is not a matter of fixating on a special locus and deliberately focusing attention there. It is nothing more than using emptiness and stillness to return the spirit to the inside.

Generally speaking, the mind of an ordinary person just races around outside day in and day out. All of its external devices and skills are only visible reflections of the light of spirit. If your spirit is wholly directed to attention on externals, then you are not aware of your own self.

Right now, you needn't search elsewhere or seek afar. Just

take the externally focused spirit and collect it back in, letting go of all mechanical cleverness, single-mindedly storing it inside, eliminating mixed-up thoughts. This is reversing the gaze to illumine inwardly. In reality, the gaze gazes on nothing; the illumination illumines nothing; and yet there is never lack of insight and perception.

Throughout the whole human body, there is only one basic energy, without distinction of heart, liver, spleen, lung, kidney, or genital energies. Ordinary people, however, are subject to compulsions of senses and objects, so this energy drifts and disperses externally. Alchemy involves no other skill but turning the light around to reverse the gaze and collecting this energy into the most recondite depths; after a long time, creativity will take place spontaneously therein.

Beginning work on turning the light around to illumine inwardly

The *Tao Te Ching* says, "Concentrating your energy, making it supple, can you be like an infant?"

The Master of Eternal Spring said, "It is just a single spiritual efficacy, without any mixed thoughts, like an infant with no conception of externals."

The Preserver of Truth said, "Concentrating energy and making is supple is a matter of forgetting emotional consciousness. The shortcut to forget emotional consciousness is in mind and breathing resting on each other. If the mind and the breathing are always resting on each other, then emotional consciousness is naturally forgotten without trying to forget."

Immortal Sister Ho said, "The stem of life is in the true breath."

The "Womb Breath" section of the *Jade Classic of Supreme Purity* says, "When you are in your mother's belly before being born, you breathe along with your mother without seeing or hearing; there is just breath there. Then when you are born and the umbilical cord is cut, the point of real basic energy masses under the navel. Day after day the spirit goes out, energy shifts, and eventually you no longer preserve the breath that was there in the womb."

The *Collection of Transmissions of the Way* says, "What you exhale is your own basic energy, emerging from within; what you inhale is the wholesome energy of heaven and earth, coming in from outside. If the root source is stable and the basic energy is not diminished, then the wholesome energy of heaven and earth can be absorbed in the interval of a breath. If, however, the root source is not stable, vitality is exhausted and energy weak, your basic energy leaks and your chamber of the fundamental goes unrepaired. The wholesome energy of heaven and earth you breathe in leaves with exhalation, while the basic energy in your body does not remain your own but is taken away by heaven and earth."

The *Treatise on the Womb Breath* says, "If you breath out without having spiritual mastery, then the one breath is incomplete; if you breathe in without mastering spirit, the one breath is incomplete then too."

Yu Yuwu said, "Throughout the twenty-four hours of the day, just cause the mind to drive the energy at all times, so that energy and spirit combine; then the physical body will survive."

He also said, "The essential thing is to keep the spirit and the breathing resting on each other, with energy and spirit keeping each other at all times."

He also said, "The method of alchemy is to have creative active energy descend to mix with receptive passive energy, cause the outbreath and inbreath to unite, and make firmness and flexibility match and mate as husband and wife, making them a unity. Then spirit and energy return to the root, essence and life join as one, and the ultimate elixir is conceived therein."

He also said, "After all, it is no more than a matter of mind and breath resting on each other, such that there is inner sensing of yin and yang and the combining of spirit and energy."

The *Four Hundred Words on Alchemy* says, "When spiritualized energy enters the root, if closure is extreme you err on the side of intensity, while if relaxation is extreme you err on the side of carelessness. Just bring about a fine continuity, not allowing interruption. After that the spirit will eventually congeal on its own, and the breath will eventually settle on its own."

Su Dongpo said, "The method of following the breath is to go out with the breath and in with the breath; follow it continuously, and one breath abides. You may feel this breath coming from the pores; clouds evaporate, fog disperses, illnesses disappear, obstructions vanish, and you spontaneously realize clear understanding."

Zhu Huai's *Guide to Tuning the Breathing* says, "When quiescence reaches a climax and you are empty, this is like a spring pond in which the fish become still after movement, like insects in hibernation; with living energy opening and closing, the wonder is inexhaustible."

Chao Wen said, "When mind and breath rest on each other, the mind becomes calm and the breathing regular; eventually this can produce superior concentration. When spirit and energy combine, spirit is harmonious and energy is clear; harmony and clarity eventually can bring about prolongation of life."

Point to the Mystery says, "Just manage to be aware,

breath after breath; this will exchange the physical body, a flow of liquid jade."

Chen the Blank said, "Breath after breath returning to the root is the matrix of the pill of gold."

The Preserver of Truth said, "When the breath makes a sound as it goes in and out, that is called carelessness; when exhalation and inhalation are not thorough, this is called stagnation. When there is repeated shortness of breath, this is called panting. Not careless, not stagnating, not panting, continuously present, working without strain—this is called breathing. Carelessness results in scattering; stagnation results in binding; panting results in laboring; maintaining 'breathing' results in stabilization. So-called tuning the breathing simply means seeing to it that you are not careless, not stagnating, and not panting."

Tuning the breath is beginner's work. Ordinarily people's minds and thoughts have rested on things, both abstract and concrete, and have been stuck to them so long that if they were to detach from objects, they would be unable to stand on their own; and even if they can stand on their own temporarily, before long they revert to a state of distraction and scatteredness. That is why the method of mind and breath resting on each other is used: to control the mind in order to refine away its coarseness. Once you get the mind detached from objects, then just be empty; you don't need to tune the breathing anymore.

If you manage to reach the state where there is no sky and no earth, no self and no other, then what breath is there to tune? This method is the most rapid shortcut, the easiest and most benign, unlike methods such as keeping the mind on the "elixir field" in the lower abdomen or the "central yellow" in the thorax. It is a reliable basis of practice. The Meditation Master of Essential Emptiness said, "In people of the highest potential, if thoughts do not arise, it is not even necessary to pay attention to the breath. But if you notice a thought arising, just tune the breath once, paying attention to it for the moment and stopping when there is no thought. Don't focus attention too intensely!"

Autumn Cicada Liu's *Secrets of Realization* says, "Gradually concentrate energy to make it unresisting. As soon as you sense your breathing unresistant and gentle, this is return to the root. I call this return to the ocean of the fundamental. When you sense return to the ocean of the fundamental with certitude, then forget it. Forget without oblivion, perceiving it mentally."

The Master of Complete Unity said, "If you use attention, that's not forgetting; if you forget, you cannot perceive mentally. So it seems that these two cannot be combined, doesn't it?" The Meditation Master of the Peak of the Center said, "Total presence of mind is called 'perceiving'; utter disappearance of whims is called 'forgetting.' Forgetting and perceiving are one yet two, two yet one. When you forget, your mind is profoundly calm and ever perceptive; when you perceive, nothing stands on its own, and all is ever forgotten. This is true forgetfulness and true perception. Many have constrained perception by speaking only of mentally perceiving!"

Secrets of Realization says, "If you become oblivious or distracted by going along with perception, this is the extreme of emptiness. This is serious, this is dangerous—you need to be guarded and calm, as everything acts up at once."

The Master of Complete Unity said, "The extreme of emptiness means that people are ordinarily so scattered in a thousand thoughts and myriad cogitations that the home has no master; it is as if deserted. If you suddenly try to collect it, you cannot hold it steady, and you are unable to be serene;

that is why you become confused along with perception. This is not merely a matter of oblivion and distraction: once this thought is let loose, there is nowhere it won't go—that is why it says 'everything acts up at once.' "

"The way to cure this is to melt falsehood the moment you sense random movement, and return to reality. The way to return is simply to forget deliberate attention to perception.

"This exercise is the mainspring of movement and stillness, the teaching of gathering in the spirit as soon as it goes out. When you come to this, just beware of not maintaining alertness."

Secrets of Realization says, "If you are unable to overcome something by perception, then dismiss it by adaptive response. Once the adaptive response is done, then forget it."

The Master of Complete Unity said, "When, as it says, 'everything acts up at once,' then whether you are active or at rest, you perceive this consciously. If you are too scattered, the power of conscious perception is incapable of calm independence. If you then attempt forced repression, that will lead to greater excitement and unease. Therefore you should employ other means, adapting responsively until things gradually settle down on their own.

"In Chan Buddhism, for example, besides sitting meditation there is prostration, scripture recitation, and walking meditation; all of them are for overcoming obstructions, and they should not be done with excessive intensity. One should ease up a bit, to gradually get a balance between relaxation and hurry. When dealing with things adaptively, if you do not flow along with the movement, you overcome obstacles. When you have attained some peace and equilibrium, then forget it while yet being aware of it."

Secrets of Realization says, "Just remain on the brink of

existence in all activities, a fine continuity, spirit and energy resting on each other in the primordial state before the absolute, uninterrupted."

The Master of Complete Unity said, "All activities means walking, standing, sitting, and reclining. Remaining on the brink of existence means that consciousness is centered. Spirit and energy resting on each other in the primordial state before the absolute depicts the state in the womb before birth, where there is neither emotion nor knowledge, but only pure unadulterated wholeness. Only when you reach this point can you recognize it."

Secrets of Realization says, "Remain centered, thus bringing about harmony, and desires will not be able to move you. If desires cannot move you, then energy embraces spirit. When spirit and energy follow each other, spirit is clear, energy peaceful, and you enter into the Vastness."

The Master of Complete Unity said, "This 'center' is most difficult to describe; it's not that there is a central location. In reality it just requires this state not to be shaken or stirred, profoundly calm and serene, naturally bringing about harmony and not being moved. This exercise is called embracing the basic and maintaining unity."

The Womb Breath

The *Triplex Unity* says, "Exhalation and inhalation nurture each other; stilling the breath, they become husband and wife."

The *Treatise on the Womb Breath* says, "Spirit and energy join and preserve the internal breath."

Yu Yuwu said, "The universe breathes within; that is why

it endures. If people can breathe internally like the universe, they too can endure as long as the universe."

The *Collection of Great Works on Alchemy* says, "Breathing out, heart and lungs; breathing in, liver, kidneys, and genitals. Breathing out, you contact the root of heaven; breathing in, you contact the root of earth. Breathing out, the dragon howls and clouds rise; breathing in, the tiger roars and wind rises."

The *Southern Flower Classic* says, "Complete people breathe from their heels."

The *Classic of the Yellow Court* says, "Behind, there is a secret door; in front, the gate of life. Exhaling the sun, inhaling the moon, respiration remains."

Some ask where the place of respiration of real people is. Liao Zhanhui said, "Opposite the navel in front and the kidneys in back, in the center there is the true gold crucible; this is the place of real breathing."

Fan Dezhao the Illumined said, "When inner energy does not go out and external energy does not come in, that does not refer to holding your breath"

Nowadays many speak of tuning the breath, and some teach people to hold their breath. Is this correct? No! *The Secret of the Sacred Embryo* says, "One energy masses in the ocean of energy, and the genital energy does not rise; then the breath stabilizes."

Generally speaking, when you tune your breathing for a long time, the longer you do it, the more solidified your spirit and the more subtle your breathing. Eventually there is no breathing in the nose, just a subtle breath coming and going over the navel, like a fetus in the womb. That is why it is called womb breathing.

This is great stabilization of spiritualized energy; it occurs naturally, not by deliberate holding and forced stopping or any other contrived means. As long as people congeal the spirit without thought, they will not fail to accord.

If emotionalized perception is not forgotten, thoughts go on and on, and the spirit is neither stable nor calm; then there are countless difficulties, and no one can attain the marvel. So it was said by Master Yuan of the Cosmic Void, "What is essential is to work on forgetting machinations and cutting off thoughts." Master Siao the Realized said, "Maintain oneness, and breath does not come and go." *The Secret of the Sacred Embryo* says, "A single thought does not arise; a single idea does not stir; there is not the slightest miss at all." How could this refer to control and suppression?

Practical refinement must reach womb breathing before energy returns to the ocean of the fundamental; this is the process of "gestation." If you close your eyes and keep silent, yet you breathe through your mouth and nose as ever, then your spiritual energy is still leaking; when the period of gestation is done, there will be no emerging and flourishing of energy and growth. The Master of Eternal Spring said, "The slightest lack of stability in the breath, and your life is not your own."

The primal

The *Triplex Unity* says, "Wholeness goes right into nonresistance."

It also says, "A primal whole, female and male go along with each other."

Yu Yuwu said, "There is no other act to cultivating refinement than culling primal unified energy for the matrix of the elixir."

He also said, "Spirit concentrates, energy collects, and they merge into one: inwardly you do not sense your body; outwardly you are not conscious of the universe. As you merge with the Way, myriad cogitations disappear, leaving an undefinable, indescribable state, which might be called 'absolute unity.'"

When practical cultivation reaches the womb breath, then the eight energy channels all become still, and you enter into undifferentiated wholeness. This is precisely the time of "intercourse." The energies of the five elements of the body meet in the elixir field. This is called gathering the five elements and combining the four forms. This is called absolute unity containing true energy; this is called the primal unified energy. Cultivation must reach this stage before you can penetrate heaven and earth and take over creative evolution.

It is impossible, however, to reach the marvels of heaven and earth without utter emptiness and quietude. That is why ancient wizards said, "Do not seek Creation in the loins; seek the Primal in the heart."

The arising of positive energy

The *Triplex Unity* says, "Imbued with the original, empty and unattached, plant vitality in the offspring."

Yu Yuwu said, "The marvel of the gold elixir is conceived in the primal and born in the temporal. What is the primal? Tranquil and unstirring, profound abstraction prior to the differentiation of the absolute. What is the temporal? Sensitive efficacy, ecstatic buoyancy, after the differentiation of the absolute. The primal is just one energy; in the temporal it subsequently turns into true vitality."

The Master of Silent Sunlight said, "The primal is the reality of pure creativity, pure positive energy. The temporal is the product of basic original vitality, so it is called *water*. Primal basic energy is the true energy of the sacred father and sacred mother: what is produced is basic original vitality, not basic original energy."

The Master of True Sunlight said, "The true energy latent in the genitals is called lead. In the energy is the water of true unity, referred to as the tiger, which is the silver in lead. Genital energy is transmitted to liver energy; liver energy is transmitted to heart energy; heart energy, by way of the absolute, becomes liquid. This is called cinnabar. The presence of true positive energy in the liquid is called the dragon, which is the mercury in cinnabar."

In these terms, the primal basic energy in the genitals is true lead yang, while the basic vitality is silver tiger yin. The liquid in the heart is cinnabar yin; the wholesome positive energy in the liquid is mercury dragon yang. Once the basic original vitality has risen, then it can keep the wholesome positive energy stable. This is what Master Zhongli referred to as beginning by using yin to keep yang. Old wizards used to generally call this true lead controlling mercury; this deserves careful thought.

Culling

The Master of True Sunlight said, "When transmission is carried out, govern it methodically. Cause genital energy not to run out, and cull the water of true unity; see to it that the heart liquid isn't wasted away, and cull from the liquid wholesome positive energy."

Master Ziyang said, "Culling means gathering true lead from the genital region and taking true mercury from the heart field."

Verses on Restoring Life says, "Culling requires intimate communion and truthful discernment. It is most difficult to find the channel of intent; it is easy to lose the cold spring."

Ziyang's *Alchemical Directions* says, "The method of culling is born in the mind; you need to forget it before you seek." It also says, "Seek in forgetting, forget in seeking; cull in forgetting, forget in culling."

Chen the Blank said, "When body and mind are unmoving, that is culling medicine."

Originally there was no "culling" in the science of wizardry, but there is a resemblance to culling in the use of true lead in the genitals and the use of true mercury in the heart. That is the only reason for the use of the term *culling*. In general, it is a matter of "gathering" without deliberate gathering, "gathering" without gathering anything; "taking" without deliberate taking, "taking" without taking anything. Don't get stuck on the imagery of these two words!

People in later times confused others even more than they had been by incoherent explanations. The ancient wizards' use of the name and image of culling was not intended to have people apply this literally. What they taught people was to be careful about function, because when positive energy first arises, it is very easily lost—if the body stirs, the energy disperses; if attention relaxes, the energy is also dispersed; if random thoughts occur, the energy is also dispersed; if you are startled or upset, the energy is also dispersed. Therefore at the time of culling it is imperative that body, mind, and attention be quiet and unstirring in order to regulate energy. Only then does primal energy come under control and does not wind up getting scattered and escaping at random. The energy then rises naturally in an orderly way, descending into the elixir field to become a supreme treasure. This is evidently what Chen the Blank meant when he said, "Body and mind unmoving is culling medicine." It does not refer to toilsome exercises in imagination and visualization!

Keeping the attention on heaven

Yu Yuwu said, "In the primal, congeal the spirit in the Earth umbilicus to produce medicine; in the temporal, shift the spirit into the Heaven cauldron to make the elixir."

He also said, "From morning to evening, the basic spirit resides in Nirvana."

The Master of Complete Unity said, "This is called the key at the crown; this is how energy is caused to rise."

The Master of the Cosmic Void said, "From ancient times to now, who does not know that the mind is the house of the spirit—so how can people talk about the spirit residing in Nirvana? This is a mistake resulting from misunderstanding of pictorial images of wizardry."

Actually, Nirvana is the seat of purity and emptiness; the spirit residing in Nirvana means the original spirit in its immaculate purity rising above and beyond vitality and energy; it does not mean dwelling in the brain.

In wizardry, Heaven is the mind and Earth is the body. Congealing the spirit in the Earth umbilicus is the beginning of alchemy: it is just a matter of congealing the spirit, whereupon energy spontaneously returns to the body and eventually flows naturally into the genital region.

It is like turbid water wherein the sediment eventually sinks on its own; it is not a matter of fixed concentration. At this time there is just a spiritual brilliance: when you sense this energy returning to the ocean of the fundamental, this is perceiving it without ever having used any deliberate effort to do so. As long as you keep aware of it this way, the energy will stay below, unable to rise, so at this time it is imperative to forget and no longer watch it. Then the true fire emerges spontaneously, and true yin rises naturally.

When the spirit returns to the crimson chamber of the heart, it is effortless and natural, so it is called shifting the spirit into the Heaven crown. Again, this does not mean that the spirit dwells in the Nirvana chamber in the brain. During the process of incubation, the spirit is always effortless; energy rises and descends naturally, without dwelling on the Nirvana chamber morning and night.

The various metaphors and pictorial representations used in wizardry became the objects of fixations. People eventually clung to the Nirvana chamber to the point where they confusedly got involved in deliberate intentional attempts to produce inner movements of energy, not realizing themselves what they were doing.

The Preserver of Truth said that the issue of whether mind can drive energy is a matter of whether or not it can manage the job, not a matter of where it abides. When an emperor rules a whole continent, does he have to preside personally over each and every locality to maintain order? The path of refining the spirit values having no fixations: to rest the spirit in the Nirvana chamber is to cling to the Nirvana chamber. This might be called a technique of moving energy, but as refinement of the spirit, I don't know—it actually disturbs the spirit!

The rising and descending through the three chambers spoken of by the ancients is spontaneous rising and descending, not rise and descent caused by the person. What they called the operation of the cycle is spontaneous operation, not an operation carried out by the person.

The central path

The *Triplex Unity* says, "Transformative action circulates everywhere; contraction and expansion repeat over and over."

It also says, "If you practice this unremittingly, clouds and rain of abundant energy will overflow like a pond in spring, liquid as melting ice. From the head it flows to the feet, then ultimately rises again, coming and going, penetrating limitlessly, passing through the center of the valley."

Yu Yuwu said, "The essential task of alchemy is to open the passive and active energy channels. That is because these two channels, the passive and the active, are the body's oceans of yin and yang. If people can open these, then all channels will open, resulting in unobstructed circulation through the body. The central path in the body is the proper route of rise and descent of yin and yang through the body; opening it up is not an exercise of energy, not a visualization, not metallic vitality, and not exercising the mind, respiration, and spine. It is the Way of breathing universal harmony and preserving the truly basic."

Opening the passive and active energy channels is the greatest marvel of the Sect of Life. Because the energy of Heaven operates unceasingly, Earth does not collapse; by virtue of unceasing operation of energy in the human being, the physical body does not decay. That operation is natural, spontaneous operation, not the operation of breathing exercises with all that squeezing and stretching, huffing and puffing. This seems to be what is meant by the saying, "A hinge pivot does not rot; flowing water does not go stale."

Jiang of the Green Mist said, "The human body is major yang in the left foot and major yin in the right foot, while in the soles of the feet is the Welling Spring, which gives forth two energies, watery and fiery, which go from the feet into the coccyx and rise to join the twofold kidney: the left to the hall of the kidneys, the right to the seat of vitality. One is watery, one fiery; one is a tortoise, one a snake. Together they foster each other and thus rise up the spine, through twenty-four vertebrae, combining in the seat of wind and rising to the Nirvana chamber, descending from Nirvana to the Hall of Brightness, then dispersing to irrigate the five faculties, then descending the windpipe into the Crimson Chamber, and then flowing again into the original seat. Day and night the circulation flows unceasingly, all natural and spontaneous, not something done by movements of the hands and feet."

Nowadays people all drift into sidetracks; unaware of the subtle principle of spontaneous silent operation in absolute nonresistance, they misapply energy induction exercises, meditations, and visualizations to the point where they become delusional. Their aberrant practices have the negative effect of producing sickness. The jaundice found among followers of the White Lotus Path and the bloating seen among followers of energetics are both evidences of this.

The firing process

Hu the Whole said, "This fire erupts in the ecstasy of true vitality, perfuming and steaming the whole body. Since it basically has no form, how can there be a process?"

Chen the Blank said, "The true fire basically has no process; the great medicine is not measured in weight."

The Master of the White Jade Moon said, "Mind is spirit; spirit is the fire. Energy is the medicine. To refine the medicine into elixir means to drive energy by spirit so as to attain the Way."

The words of these three old wizards can indeed be considered of critical importance. But driving energy by spirit requires precise clarification of the way of driving. There may be excess or insufficiency in practice: to adjust and correct this is what is called driving. This is also what is referred to as the process.

There is "no process" in the sense of no process delineated by measurements of time. There is a process in the sense of watchfulness and wariness. Only with such an understanding can we talk about the firing.

The *Triple Unity* says, "Watch with diligent care; check for cold and warmth."

Chen the Blank said, "The essential key of the firing process is to be sought in the true breath." He also said, "Positive energy arises in the ocean of the origin; fire erupts within water. The circulation of the universe and the repetition of creation are not apart from one breath."

Master Ziyang said, "Leisurely guard the medicine furnace, watching the firing process. Just settle spirit and breath, and let naturalness be so."

The firing process is all in applying effort to thought. Chen the Blank said, "Thoughts should not be aroused; if thoughts arise, the breathing is rough. Attention should not be scattered; if attention scatters, the fire goes cold."

The Old Teacher of the Open Channel to Reality said, "When thoughts arise, the breathing is rough; when breathing is rough, it blows too hard on the fire. Just tune the true breathing, causing it to be peaceful and even, avoiding agitation and excitement."

The firing process basically stands for the phases of advance and withdrawal of one energy, nothing else. When it is said that the firing has not been transmitted, that means it cannot be transmitted, not that it is kept secret. The provenience of the true fire cannot be reached by words; it is all in the human being. Generally speaking, when application of attention is too intense, this is called overheating and dryness; if too lax, this is called wetness and coldness. What you must do is find a balance of relaxation and intensity, neither forgetting nor fostering. This is the true firing process. It is said to be untransmittable because there is not a fixed rule.

When the firing process starts, human power cannot work with it; all you can do is be empty and calm and hold the rudder firmly, not letting miscellaneous thoughts disturb it. Allow it to happen naturally and spontaneously; when it has "perfumed and steamed" once, it naturally produces yin, turning into liquid that descends and irrigates the inner organs. When you have a feeling of sweet juice in your throat, that is a sign it is happening. At this point, just keep empty and calm, not disturbing it at all, and it will naturally congeal. Remain silent and still for a long time; then you may get up very, very slowly. Jiang of the Green Mist said, "When it comes, greet it with attention; when it goes, send it off with the eyes. Greeting it with attention is called the go-between; sending it off with the eyes is called the green maiden." This is mixed up in artificialities, a big mistake!

The subtlety in promoting the fire is in closing all openings tightly: if you give rise to any miscellaneous thought at all, then you are not sealed tight, and the medicine will run off.

Incubation

The *Triplex Unity* says, "The three lights submerged, incubate the seed pearl."

It also says, "Close the three treasures—ears, eyes, and mouth; do not let them act up. Real people plunge into the abyss; floating buoyantly, they keep to the compass center."

It also says, "When the fire energy works protectively within, then water needs no brilliance. Openings closed, you do not talk; speaking seldom, accord with wholeness. Once the three are locked, stay in an empty room, body relaxed, letting willfulness go, and return to absolute nonresistance. Freedom from thought is the normal experience; this is immovable. When the mind is single, it does not go wild. Sleep in the embrace of spirit; when awake, be watchful of presence and absence."

The Master of Complete Unity said, "Incubation just requires constant preservation of the true breath, causing spirit and energy to be in constant intercourse. At no time is there no true breath, so at no time is energy inoperative. Since there is no time that energy is not operating, there is no time when you are not carrying out the firing process."

Yu Yuwu said, "In quiet concentration, embrace nonresistant, harmonious energy, exhaling very subtly, inhaling very finely, up to Nirvana, down to the Gate of Life, circulating unceasingly, spirit and energy never for a moment failing to cluster together."

Punishment and reward

The *Triplex Unity* says, "Dragon east, tiger west, warp and woof, hare and cock, punishment and reward meet, joyful on seeing each other. Punishment establishes execution and restraint; reward is in charge of productivity. In the second month, the elms drop their leaves and the second Dipper star faces east; in the eighth month, wheat grows and the Dipper bowl rests in the west."

The firing process in intervals requires the concepts of the time of the hare and the time of the cock. Why do punishment and reward depend on each other? Reward is in charge of promotion and inspiration, associated with the second lunar month; punishment is in charge of execution and restraint, associated with the eighth lunar month. Punishment in the second month means descent within ascent; reward in the eighth month means ascent within descent. These images are used to symbolize potential danger. The times of the hare and the cock, dawn and dusk, refer to when ascent and descent have reached halfway, where it is easy for attention to scatter, so that ascent does not proceed upward and descent does not proceed downward. This results in stagnation that creates a lot of trouble. Therefore it is said that there is punishment in reward and reward in punishment, so that people will guard their attention as they would a citadel, not letting it scatter.

Refining the spirit

The *Book of Balance and Harmony* says, "Followers of Taoism seek lead in the seat of water; followers of Buddhism cultivate concentration in the chamber of fire."

It also says, "The upper pass is refining spirit back into emptiness. When the work reaches this point, not a single word applies."

Qing-an said, "The unique transcendental experience is to be sought outside of words. If you encounter it everywhere, realizing it and penetrating it, then returning to the perfect light of the absolute, the radiance of awareness pierces without resistance, penetrating effectively. Essence and life are both cultivated; body and spirit are both sublimated. When you are one with cosmic space, it is not hard to stand shoulder to shoulder with Wizards and Buddhas."

This passage shows the one great continuity of practical cultivation. Previous statements referred to refinement of vitality into energy; without the work of refining spirit, it will never be possible to attain transcendence. At most you might preserve your life, lengthen its span, and remedy deterioration and illness. The *Four Hundred Words on Alchemy* says, "Lead and mercury returned to the earth pot; body and mind are silent and immobile." When body and mind are unmoving, there must be that which is unmoved; unfortunately, devotees of life science do not explain it clearly. If you keep previous views, seek with greed, and become obsessively fixated, you bind yourself without rope. I'm afraid you'll be unable to see where your birth star is.

The Master of Complete Unity said, "When incubation reaches the stage of the infant manifesting form, it is still young and immature in its comings and goings, easily disturbed, still needing defense against leakage on impact. One is not yet able to 'enter the marketplace with hands extended.' "

Crystallizing the elixir

Some ask what crystallization of the elixir is. Qing-an said, "When body and mind are united, spirit and energy merged, essence and sense as one, this is called crystallization of the elixir, symbolized by the sacred embryo."

A master wizard said, "The original real essential nature is called the gold elixir pill."

Ding-an asked, "When the elixir crystallizes, is it visible?" Qing-an replied, "Yes." "Does it have form?" "No." "If it has no form, how can it be visible?" Qing-an said, "Gold elixir is just a name—how could it have form? That it is visible does not mean it can be seen with the eyes. The *Tao Te Ching* says, 'When you look at it you cannot see it; when you listen for it you cannot hear it—this is called the Way.' But even though you cannot see it when you look, never are you not seeing it; even though you cannot hear it when you listen for it, never are you not hearing it. It is not within reach of ears and eyes. It is like the wind shaking trees and raising waves—you can hardly call it nonexistent, but when you look at it you cannot see it, and when you grasp for it you cannot apprehend it, so you can hardly call it existent. The substance of the gold elixir is also like this."

Wang the Cloud Dweller said, "The substance of the gold elixir is like space, without resistance inside or out. Nothing hangs on it, nothing stains it; brilliantly luminous, it illumines infinity."

Devotees of life science all talk of cultivating vitality,

cultivating energy, producing being from nothingness, forming an infant that, born of the energy of sacred father and spiritual mother, is empty and effective, unlike a living human being. This doctrine is false.

Zhang Huangju said, "Creation gives life to people; its coming is subtle and simple, its ultimate extension vast and stable. If the infant actually had physical solidity, it would shortly be as solid as a living person—how could it be a spiritual subtlety?"

The Master of Eternal Spring said, "The 'infant' is our individual soul, our true essence, pure positive energy without adulteration. It is not that there is actually an 'infant' in the belly." He also said, "If there is the slightest confusion of thought, the spirit is not purely positive."

The Master of the White Jade Moon said, "As long as people have no mind in mind and no thought, this unadulterated clarity, immaculate, is called pure positivity."

Wizards originally just taught people to nurture the spirit, but people get lost and drown in desires and are unable to cut right through, so the notion of eternal life was set up to induce people to cultivate refinement. When worldly people crave immortality, only then are they willing to put down habitual desires and single-mindedly refine vitality and energy; so they have inner focus and think less of externals. When they have cultivated refinement to the point where energy rises and descends through the three chambers in the torso and head, the bliss felt in the body is indescribable; then they develop such a huge craving for this that they disregard everything. Here the mind has focus and gradually attains peace and quiet, so the original basic spirit gradually becomes manifest. This is the "appearance of the infant." From there, you enter into absolute nonresistance, where your mind has no attachments, myriad cogitations melt, and the basic spirit appears, coming and going freely, unobstructed by the physical body. This is transcendent liberation. In reality, this is just a matter of temporarily using refinement of vitality and refinement of energy to focus the mind and nurture the basic spirit so that it is effective.

Release from the matrix

Li Qing-an said, "Embodiment beyond the body is called release from the matrix." He also said, "When the positive spirit leaves the shell, this is called release from the matrix."

Some ask about transcendent release. The Master of the White Jade Moon said, "Transcendence means the emergence of the spirit; release means liberating change of the ordinary body."

These sayings all talk about leaving aside the ordinary body, just refining the basic spirit back into emptiness, not about maintaining a physical presence in the world. So obviously the advanced wizards did not concern themselves with immortality. Why are people today so eager for eternal life?

The following question has been posed: those who attained the Way in ancient times made even this ordinary body nonresistant, so they could enter water and fire, penetrate metal and stone, walk in space without falling, and not be blocked by contact with solidity. This is what is called the preservation of pure energy. As it is said, in disperson it is energy; in concentration it is form. This is called sublimation of body and mind, uniting with the Way. Now if one would have to relinquish the ordinary body to attain the constitution of wizardry, how could this not mean one had failed to reach sublimation of body and mind?

Master Gan of the Pure Wind said, "Before you have reached true emptiness, the yang spirit is hard to free." The Master of Eternal Spring said, "Before you have reached true emptiness, the yin spirit is also hard to free."

The ancients' liberation from the matrix and spiritualization was in every case based on the climax of emptiness and stillness, the attainment of selflessness. When people today go anywhere in dreams, it is because they are not stayed by the physical body; when they wake up, they are stuck here and cannot remove themselves to great distances because the physical body stops them. Therefore liberation from the matrix and spiritualization are possible only after true emptiness and selflessness.

It may be asked why refinement of vitality into energy does not result in transcendent liberation. Fan Dezhao's work *Accord with Reality* says, "Those who cultivate energy to take on form are yogis; even after a thousand years they still have the same old bodies and never attain the Way." Thus our Celestial Teacher said, "Even if you are long-lived as a tortoise or a crane, you are not a spiritual wizard."

In ancient times, master Qingjing, who lived for three thousand years, questioned Pengzu about sexual energetics. Asked if Qingjing were a wizard, Pengzu said, "No. A celestial dragon can form a pearl; when the pearl is done, the body spontaneously withdraws, so it is called a celestial dragon. What that adept practices is like the dragon. If you refine your body, then your spirit and energy may change to manifest the unfathomable, but this is still limited to transformation of energy. On Royal House Mountain there are accomplished Taoists of the Bone Removing Cavern who leave behind their physical bodies, because whatever has physical form cannot ascend."

Now if even a body produced by cultivation is still limited

in its energy transformations, what about the physical body inherited from your parents? Even if you have cultivated refinement to the point where you ascend to the highest heavens and live for countless years, you are still within the domain of transmutations of yin and yang and have not been able to enter into formlessness. As long as you have not entered into formlessness, you are still enslaved by the polar energies of the universe; how can there be any transcendent liberation?

Meng Yin said, "What can compare to the uncontrived entry into reality? With one leap you enter directly into the realm of the enlightened."

Returning to the origin

Is there still creative evolution after liberation from the matrix? Qing-an said, "There is still creative evolution. An ancient said, 'Embodiment beyond the body is not yet wonderful; when cosmic space itself is shattered, only then is complete reality revealed.' So after liberation from the matrix, it is essential to tread solidly on real ground; when you are one with cosmic space, that is perfect attainment."

This subject is something wizards had long left unspoken until Qing-an gave this unexpected explanation. His vision may be said to have gone beyond that of other masters. In overall terms, when you reach this stage, you have to take everything you've realized, everything you've attained, and banish it all at once to the land of birthlessness. Only then will you be in accord. If you retain any personal view of transcendent liberation, then as before you will drift into emotional consciousness, far estranged from the Way—how can you attain union with cosmic space?

Twin cultivation of essence and life

Master Zhang Ziyang said, "If you start with essence,
it's hard to apply it in practice; if you start with life,
there's a concrete way of approach. Even if the achievement
is one, nevertheless there is something better about starting
with essence."

Li Qing-an said, "The best people have already planted
roots of virtue and have inborn knowledge; once they directly
comprehend essence, they naturally comprehend life."

Essence and life are one matter. The reason people die is
that the body and spirit separate. The reason the sense organs
are useless after death even though they are still there is that
there is no spirit to manage them. Obviously the spirit is the
manager of the body; when the spirit departs, energy dissi-
pates, so how could life exist outside of essence? If you divide
them into two for twin cultivation, differentiating them into
prior and latter, that is not quite right. Why? When you cultivate essence, life is therein. As the Celestial Master of Open
Serenity said, "When spirit is restored to the body, energy
returns of itself." No one has ever been able to accomplish
intercourse to produce the elixir without being outwardly
nonresistant and serene. Indeed, first refining vitality into energy—thus cultivating stabilization and liberation from the
matrix—is roundabout and difficult to achieve fully. If you
can realize the body of reality, why worry that the physical
body will not be sublimated?

The three passes from effort to effortlessness constitute the
gradual method; cultivating the upper pass so as to include
the lower two passes is the sudden method. Now you should
directly practice refinement of spirit back into emptiness:
when you reach the state of utter emptiness and silence, vital-

ity spontaneously evolves into energy, and energy spontaneously evolves into spirit. The handle is in your grip; your
destiny is up to you. This is penetrating the three barriers
with one shot. This is simplest and easiest, most direct and
quick; those on the Way should thoroughly appreciate this.

Printed in the United States
by Baker & Taylor Publisher Services